COLORING FISH

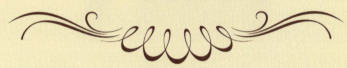

OVER 40 EXTRAORDINARY
PICTURES WITH FULL
COLORING GUIDES

ARCTURUS

This edition published in 2015 by Arcturus Publishing Limited
26/27 Bickels Yard, 151–153 Bermondsey Street,
London SE1 3HA

Copyright © Arcturus Holdings Limited

All rights reserved. No part of this publication may be reproduced, stored in a retrieval system, or transmitted, in any form or by any means, electronic, mechanical, photocopying, recording or otherwise, without prior written permission in accordance with the provisions of the Copyright Act 1956 (as amended). Any person or persons who do any unauthorised act in relation to this publication may be liable to criminal prosecution and civil claims for damages.

ISBN: 978-1-78599-245-2
AD004981US

Printed in China

Introduction

The fish of the world come in numerous and gorgeous forms, many of which are unfamiliar to us except in tropical aquaria and on our television screens—but we do have the chance to see them there. It is hard to imagine the impact that some of the more exotic species shown in these pages would have had on the majority of nineteenth-century readers, who would mainly have known only the gray and brown fish harvested from rivers and coastal waters. The illustrations here come from *The Naturalist's Library*, which was edited by the great Scottish naturalist Sir William Jardine (1800–1874) and issued in a set of 40 volumes with more than 1,300 plates engraved by his brother-in-law, William Lizars (1788–1859).

There's endless interest to be had in depicting the colors and textures of a fish's body, but it's very hard to do this from life. Working from these illustrations, you will be able to study them in detail and follow Lizars' exquisite work. And, too, you can simply revel in the pleasure of coloring in, which is now hugely popular with adults for the relaxation and satisfaction in one's skills it brings.

The choice of art materials now goes far beyond the crayons you may have used when you were a child; you can also buy oil-based, wax-based or watersoluble color pencils, colorfast and exhibition quality. You can use them dry, blending them with your finger or a paper stump, or dilute them with oil, or water for the watersoluble pencils. Alternatively, you can paint your fish—a small watercolor set and a medium-sized round brush is all you need. Whichever you choose, you'll find many hours of enjoyment from trying to match the skills of William Lizars.

Diana Vowles

Key: *List of plates*

1 *Centropristes nigricanus* (American Black Bass)

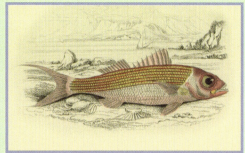
2 *Etelis carbunculus* (Ruby-colored Etelis)

3 *Apogon trimaculatus* (Mediterranean Apogon)

4 *Cheilodipterus arabicus* (Arabian Cheilodipterus)

5 *Genus perca* (Common Perch)

6 *Diploprion bifaclatum* (Two-banded Diploprion)

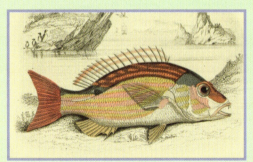
7 *Mesoprion uninotatus* (One-spotted Mesoprion)

8 *Chalceus macrolepitdotus* (Pink-tailed Chalceus)

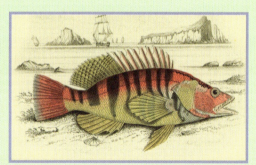
9 *Serranus scriba* (Lettered Serranus)

10 *Centrarchus cyanopterus* (Blue-finned Centrarchus)

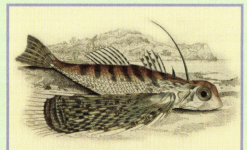
11 *Dactylopterus orientalis* (Oriental Dactylopterus)

12 *Serrasalmo niger* (Red-eyed Piranha)

13 *Exocetus volitans* (Common Flying Fish)

14 *Centrarchus cychla* (Cychla-like Centrarchus)

15 *Zanclus cornutus* (Horned Zanclus or Chaetodon)

16 *Argus pteraclis* (Pteraclis Ocellatus)

17 *Lethrynus esculentus* (Edible Lethrynus)

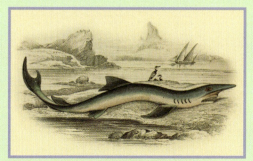
18 *Prionace glauca* (Blue Shark)

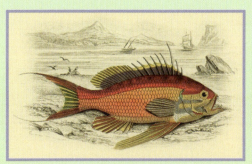
19 *Serranus anthias* (Spined Serranus)

20 *Monocentris cornutus* (Armed Monocentris)

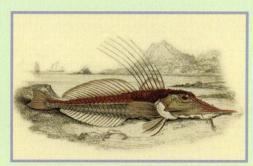
21 *Peristedion cataphractum* (Mailed Peristedion)

22 *Ostracion cubicus* (Spotted Ostracion)

23 *Acantharus hepatus* (Yellow-bellied Acanthurus)

24 *Zeus faber* (John Dory)

25 *Trachinus radiatus* (Radiated Weaver)

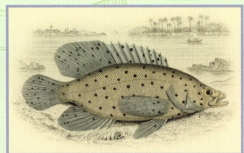
26 *Serranus altivelis* (Large-finned Serranus)

27 *Annarrhicus lupus* (Wolf Fish)

28 *Labrus mixtus* (Blue-striped Wrasse)

29 *Chimaera monstrosa* (Northern Chimaera)

30 *Labrus formosus* (Painted Labrus)

31 *Cychla rubro-ocellata* (Red-spotted Cycla)

32 *Echinorhinus spinosus* (Spinous Shark)

33 *Huro nigricanus* (The Black Bass of the Huron)

34 *Mesoprion chrysurus* (Golden-tailed Mesoprion)

35 *Acestra aequorea* (Equorcal Pipe Fish) *and Hippocampus brevirostris* (Short-nosed Seahorse)

36 *Peristedion malarmat* (Mailed Gurnard)

37 *Acerina vulgaris* (The Ruffe)

38 *Doras castaneo-ventris* (Brown Dorsal-striped Doras)

39 *Serrasalmo punctatus* (Spotted Saw-bellied Salmon)

40 *Sudis gigas* (Gigantic Sudis)

41 *Gasterosteus spinosa* (Fifteen-spined Stickleback nest and eggs)

42 *Pomatomus telescopium* (The Large-eyed Pomatome)

43 *Serrasalmo piranha* (Piranha Saw-bellied Salmon)

44 *Pimelodus insignis* (Black-spotted Green Pimelodus)

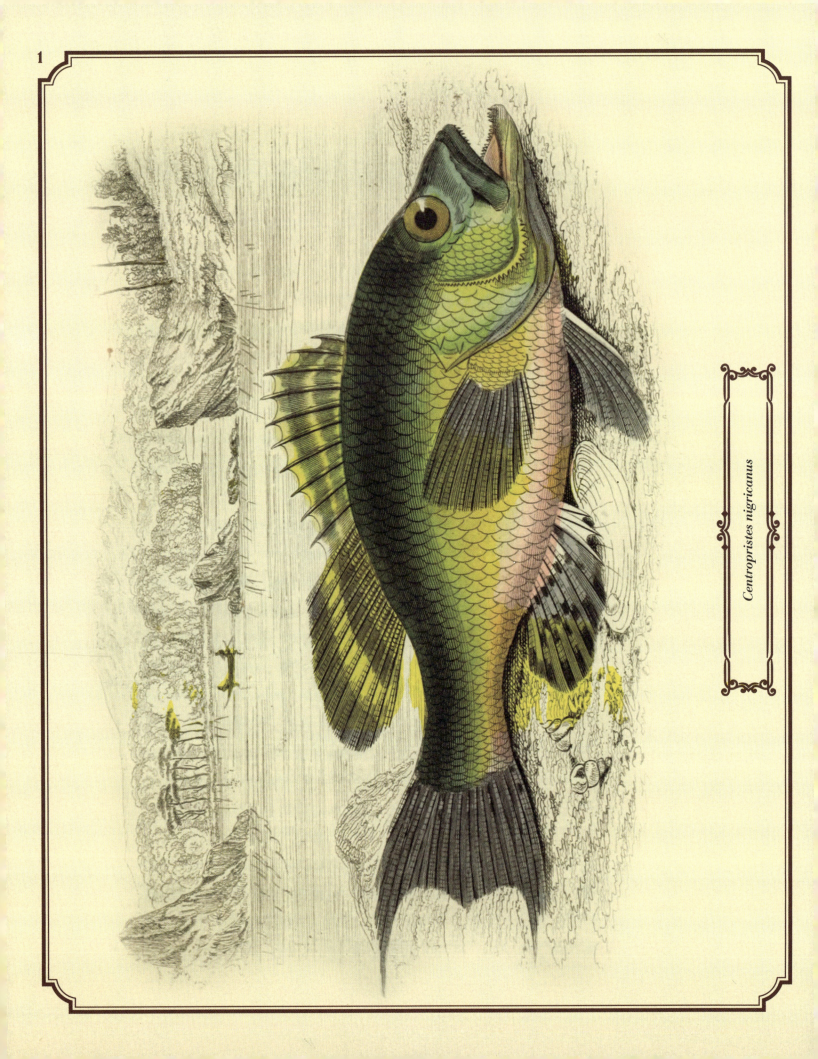

Centropristes nigricanus

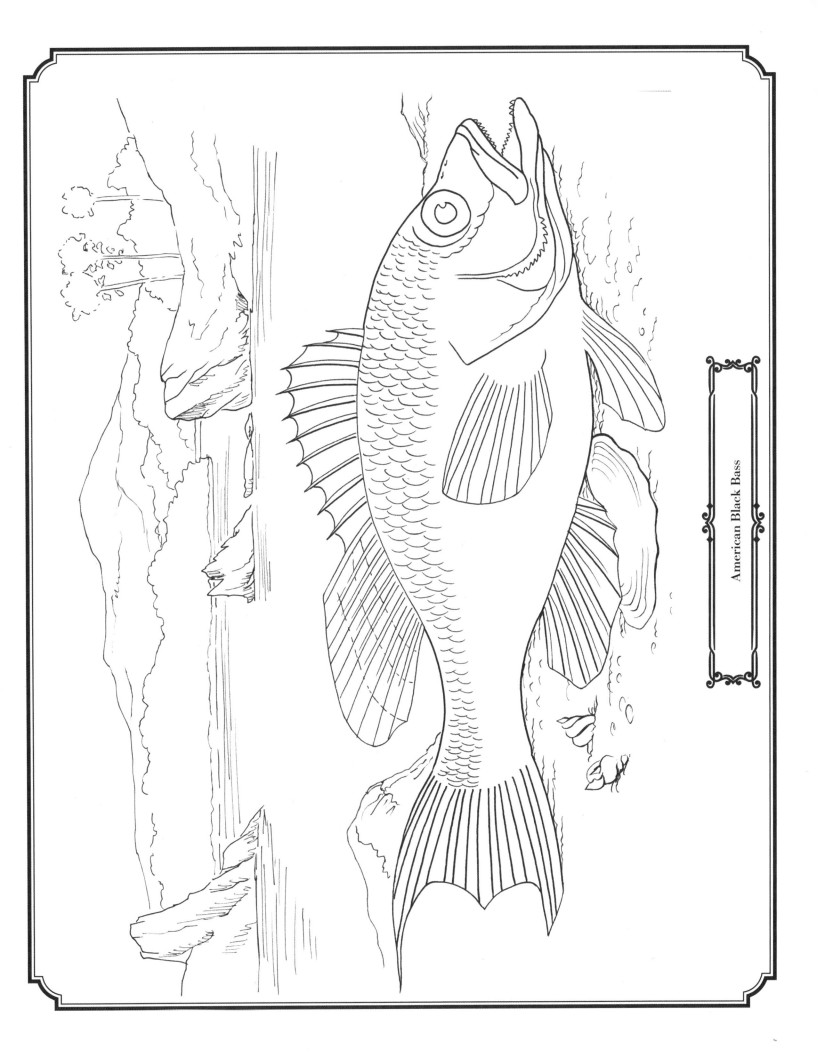

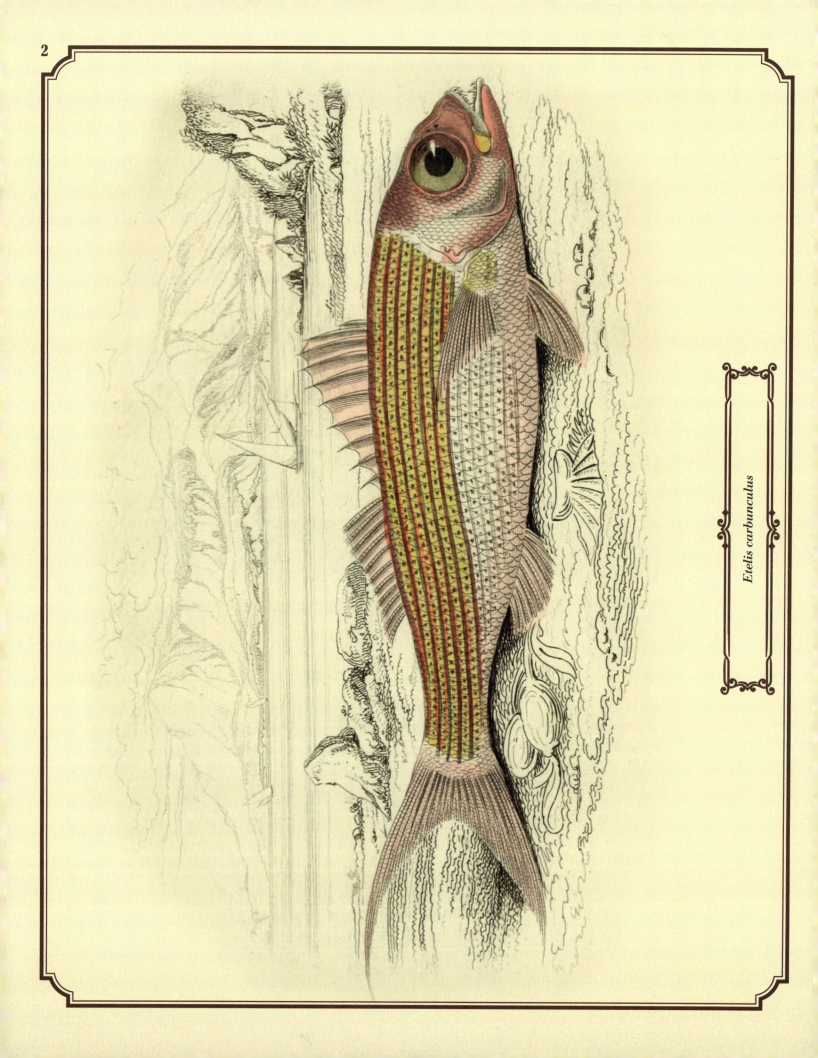

Etelis carbunculus

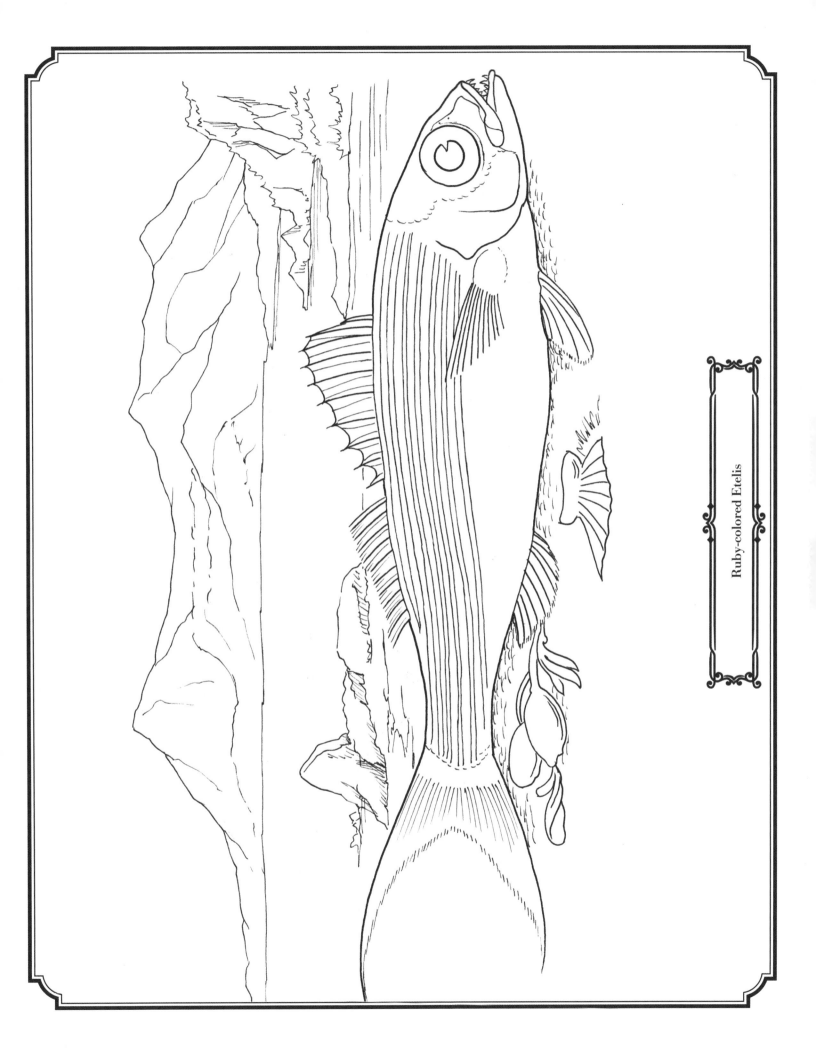
Ruby-colored Etelis

Apogon trimaculatus

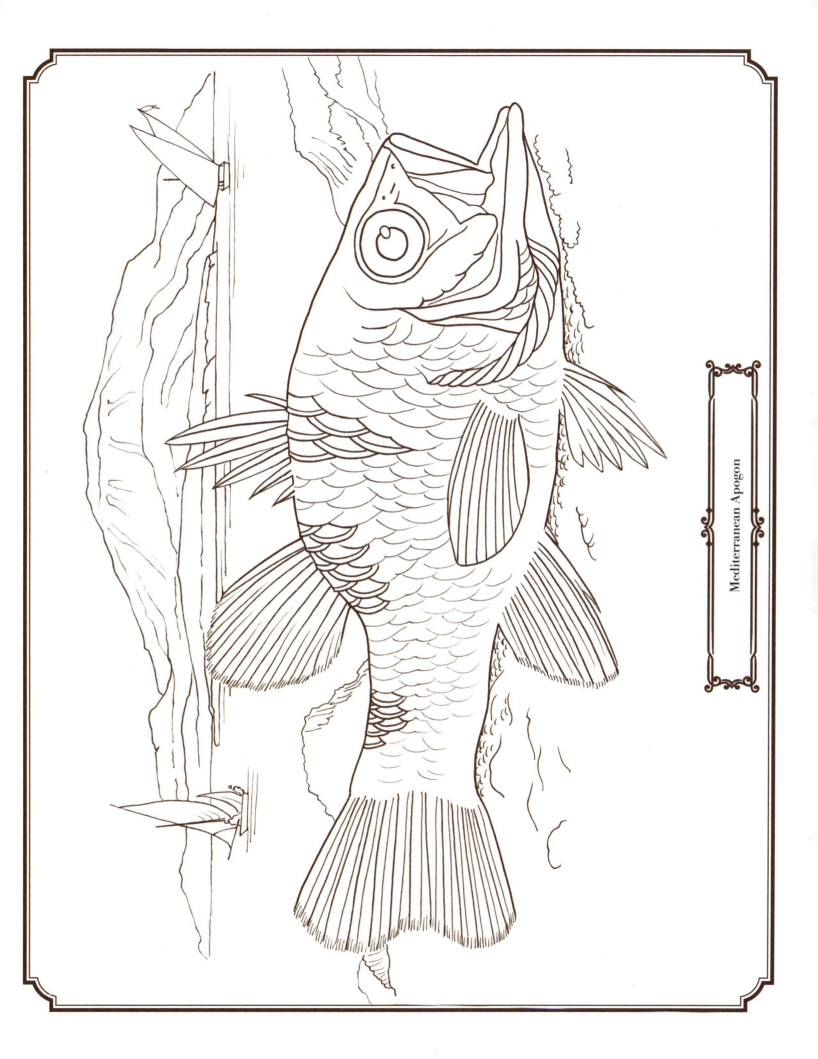
Mediterranean Apogon

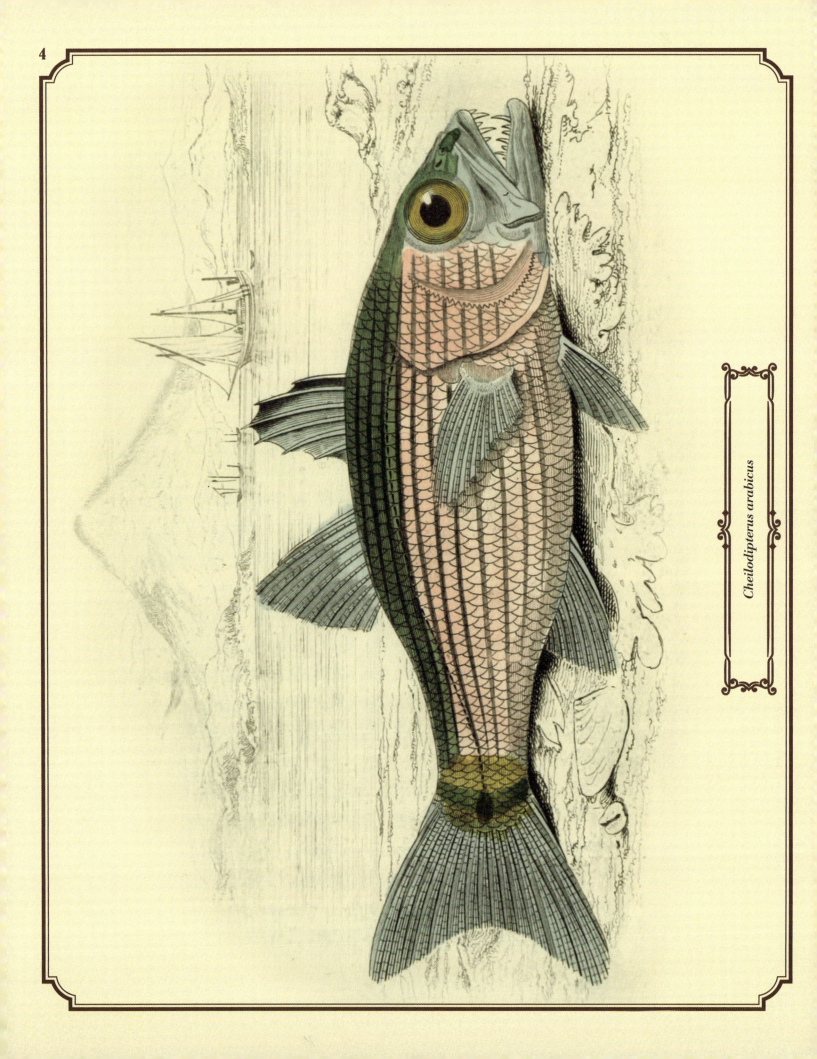
Cheilodipterus arabicus

Arabian Cheilodipterus

Genus perca

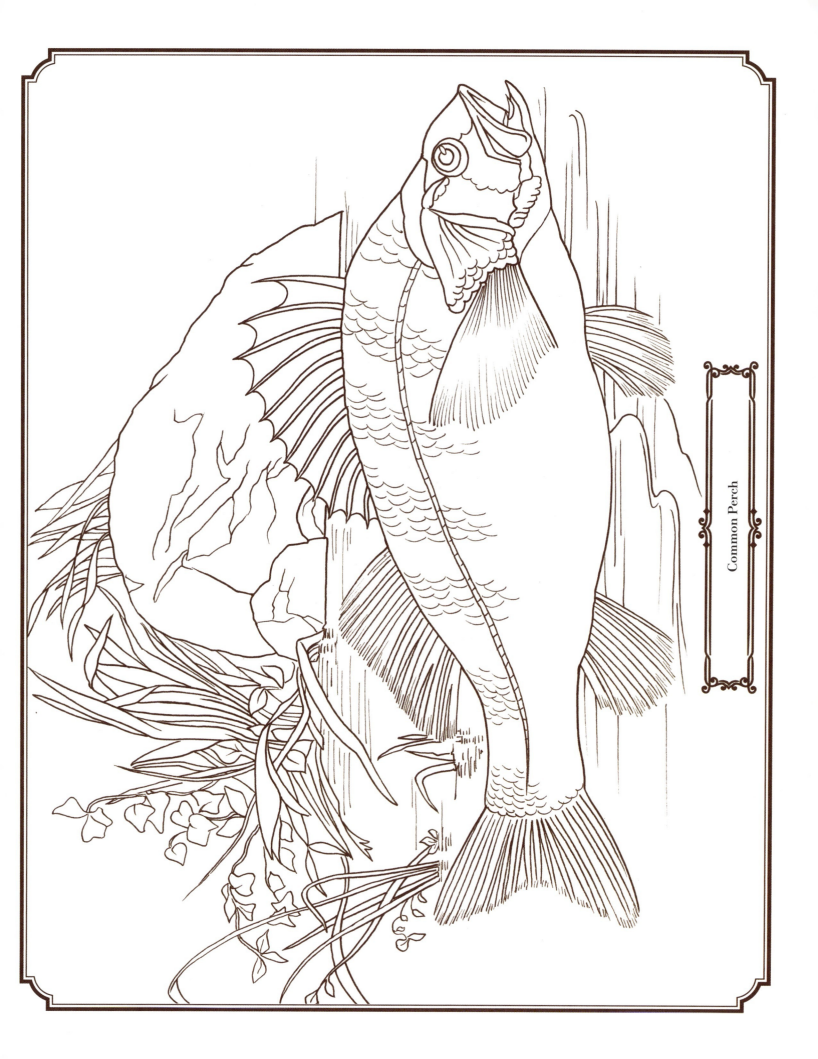

Common Perch

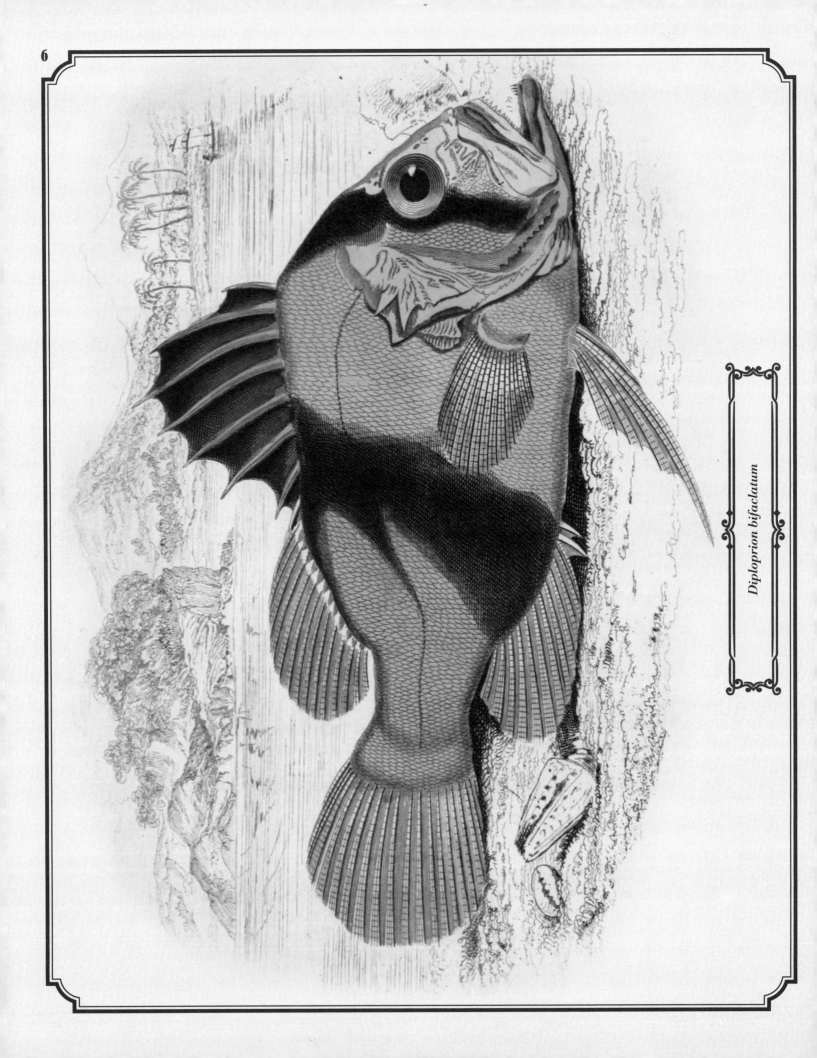
Diploprion bifaclatum

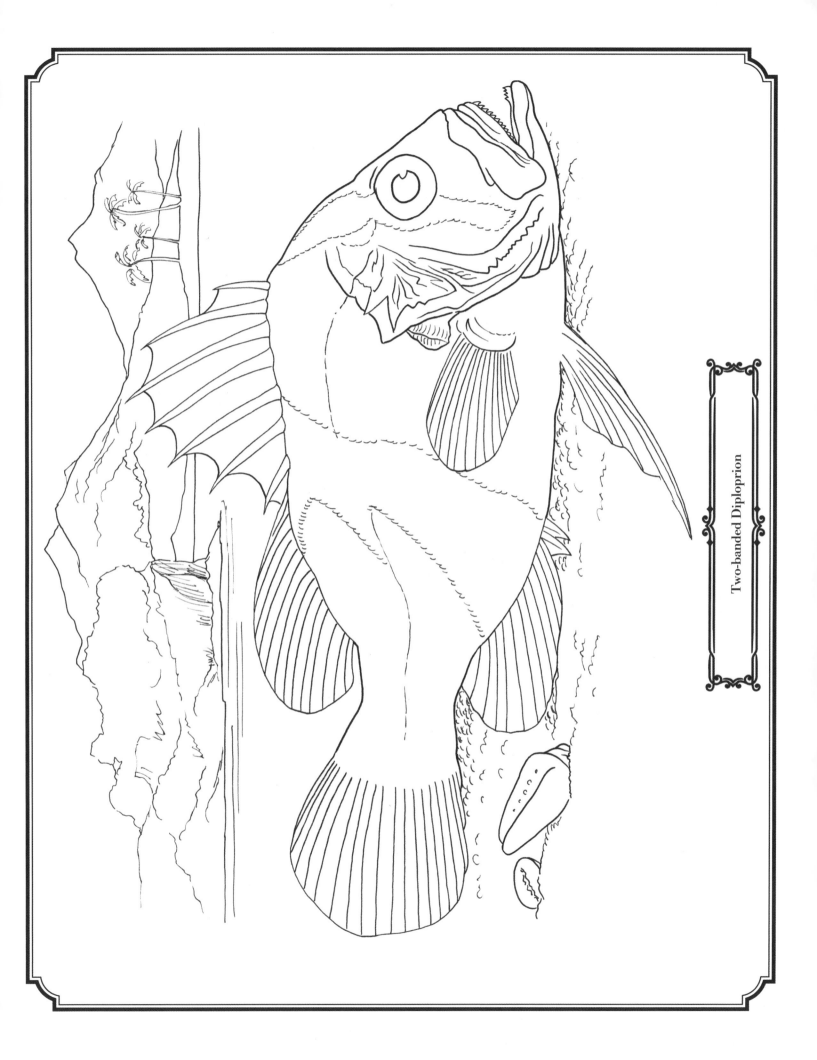

Two-banded Diploprion

Mesoprion uninotatus

One-spotted Mesoprion

Chalceus macrolepidotus

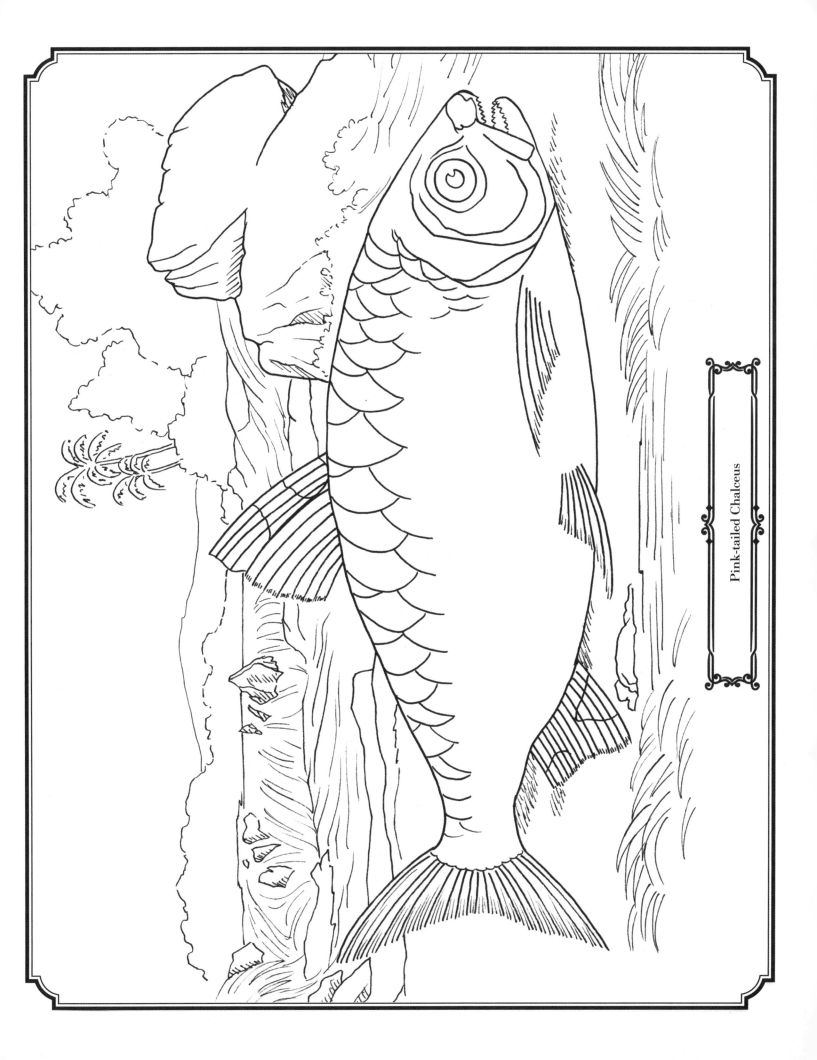
Pink-tailed Chalceus

Serranus scriba

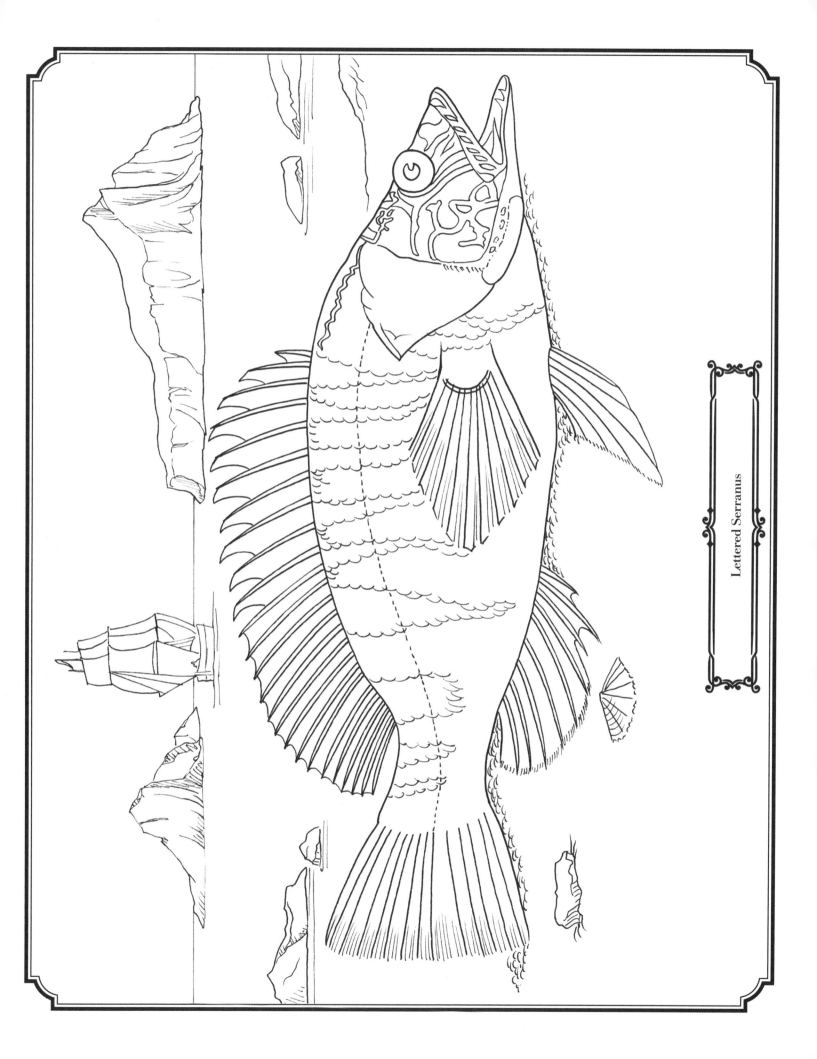

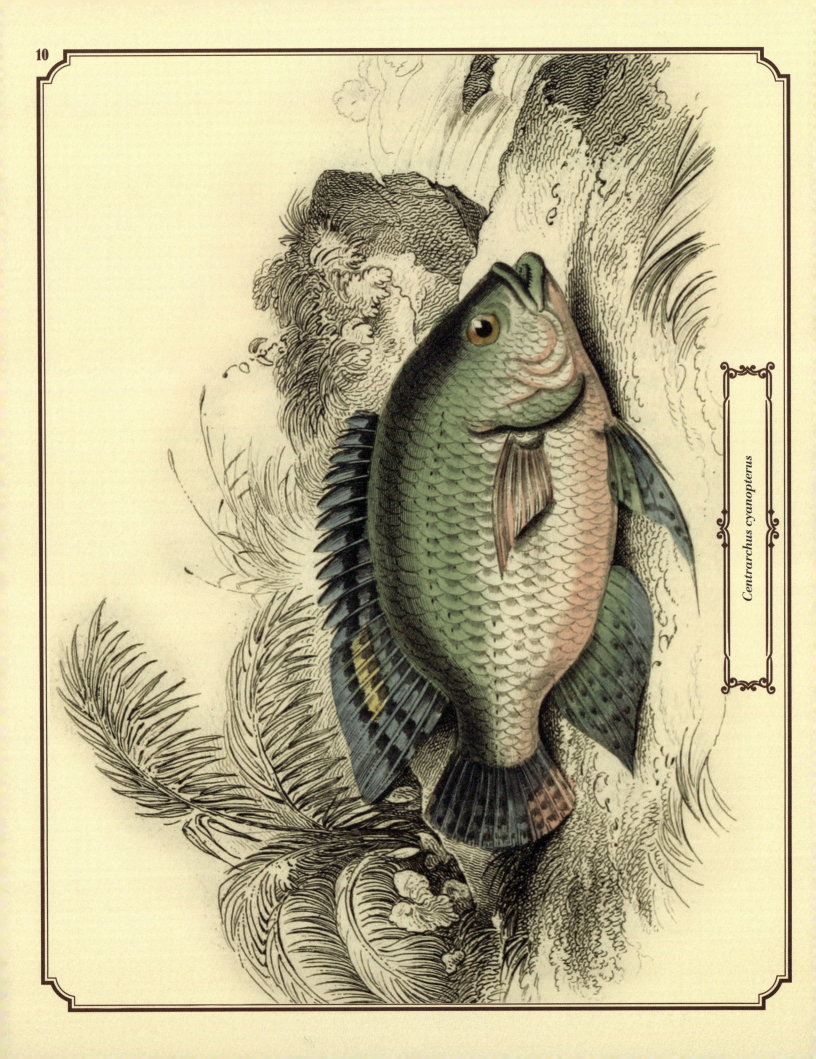

Centrarchus cyanopterus

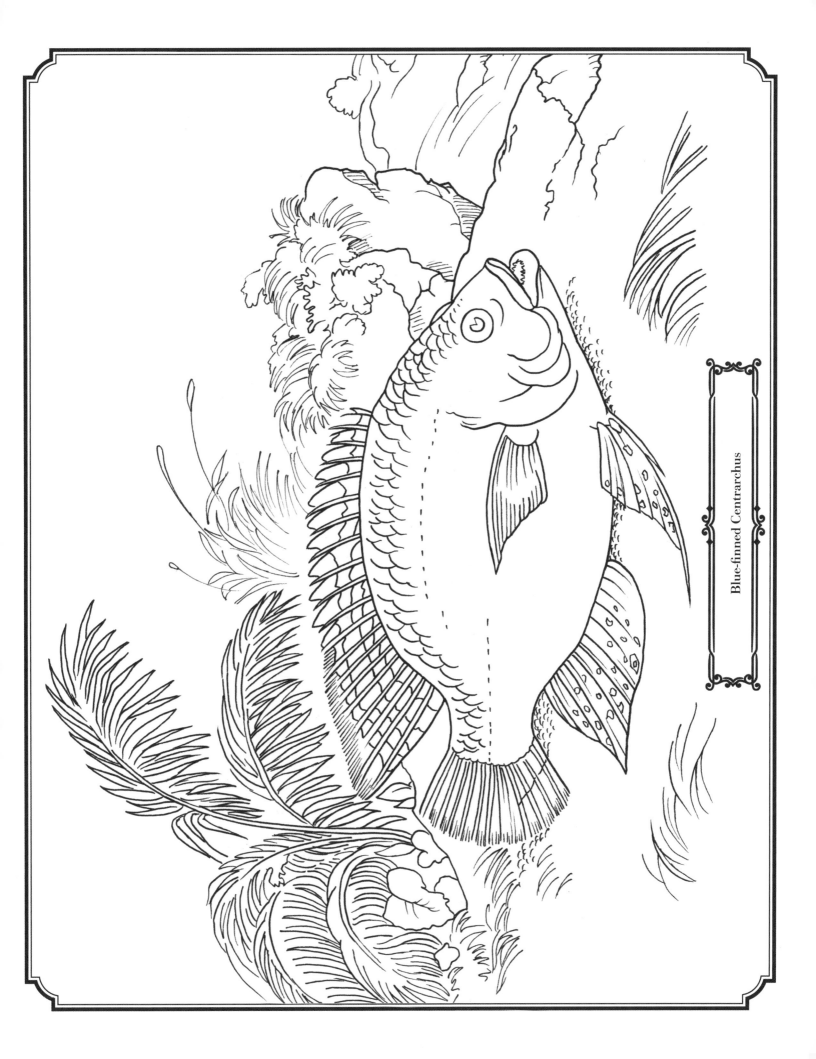
Blue-finned Centrarchus

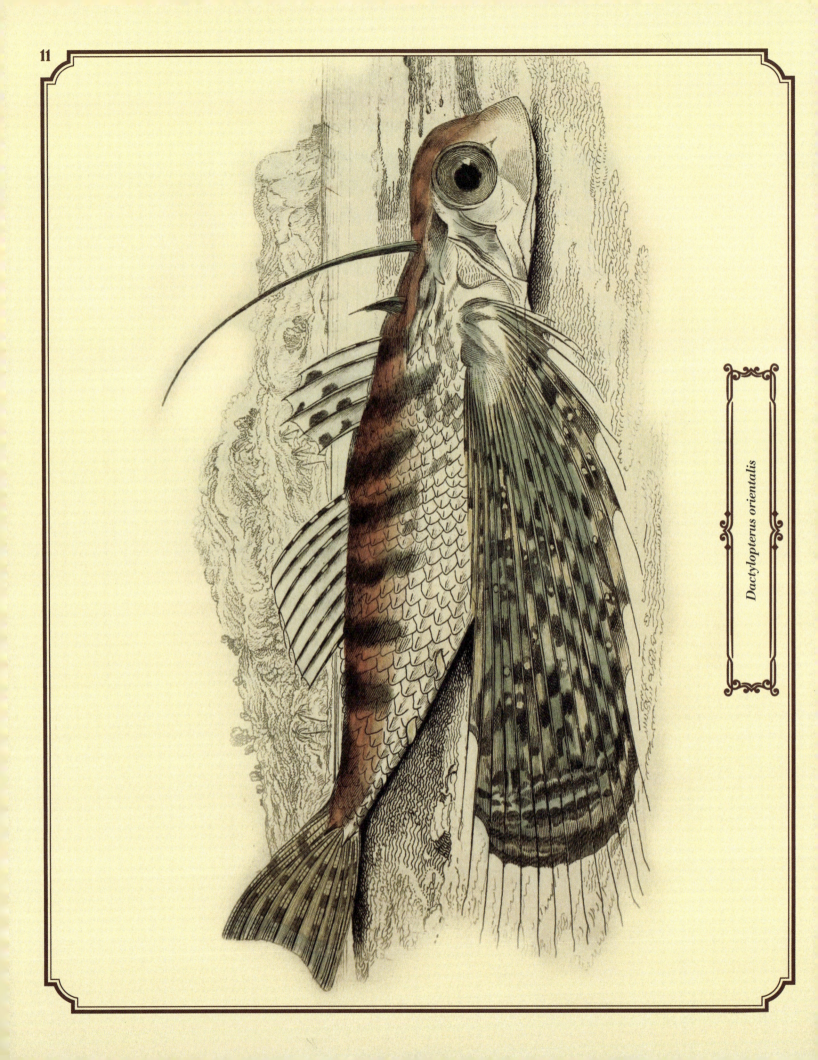

Dactylopterus orientalis

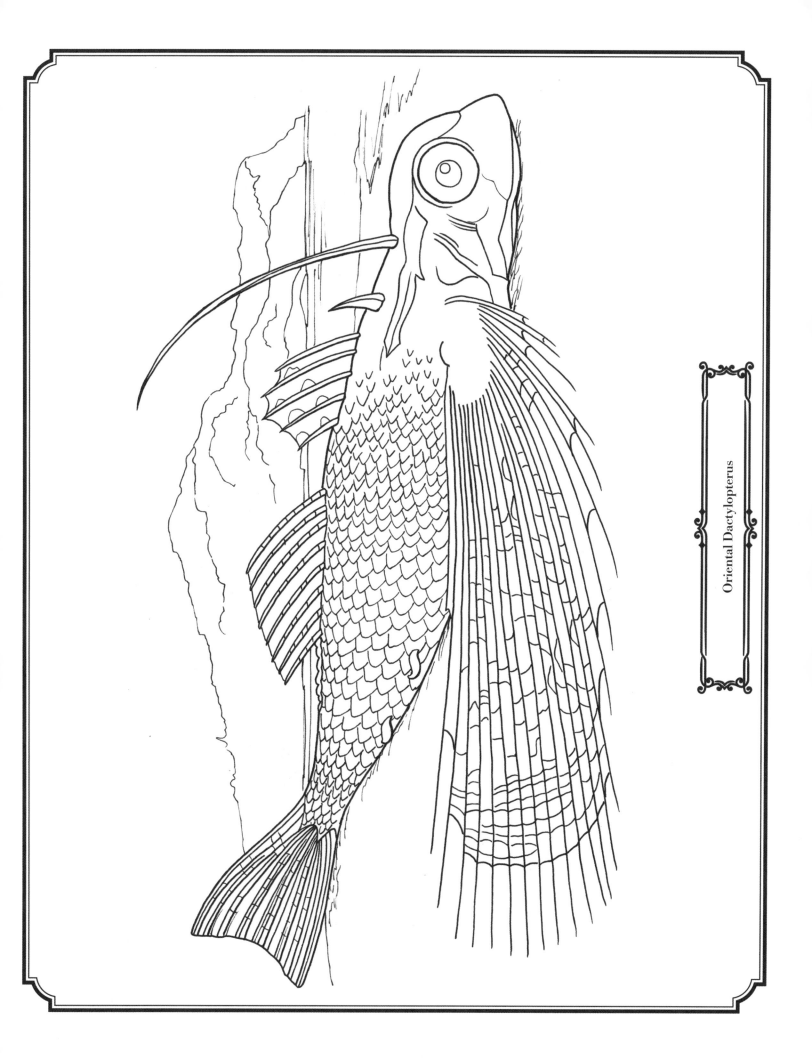

Oriental Dactylopterus

Serrasalmo niger

Red-eyed Piranha

Exocetus volitans

Common Flying Fish

Centrarchus cychla

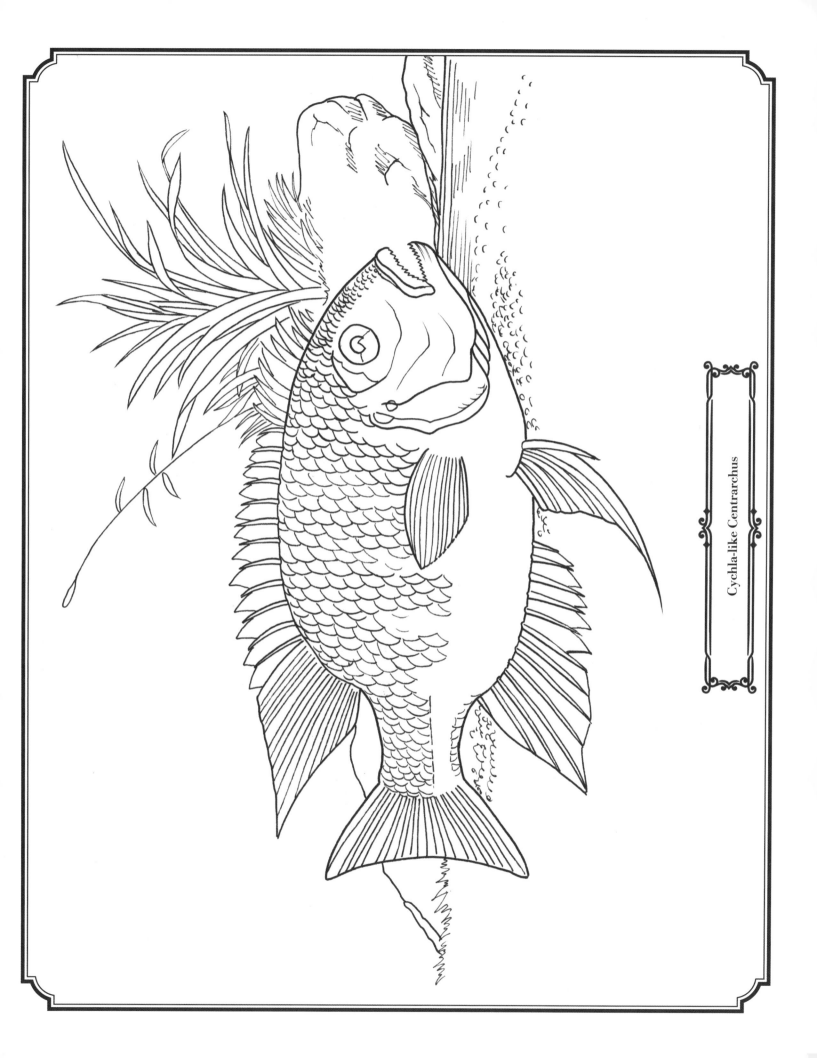

Cychla-like Centrarchus

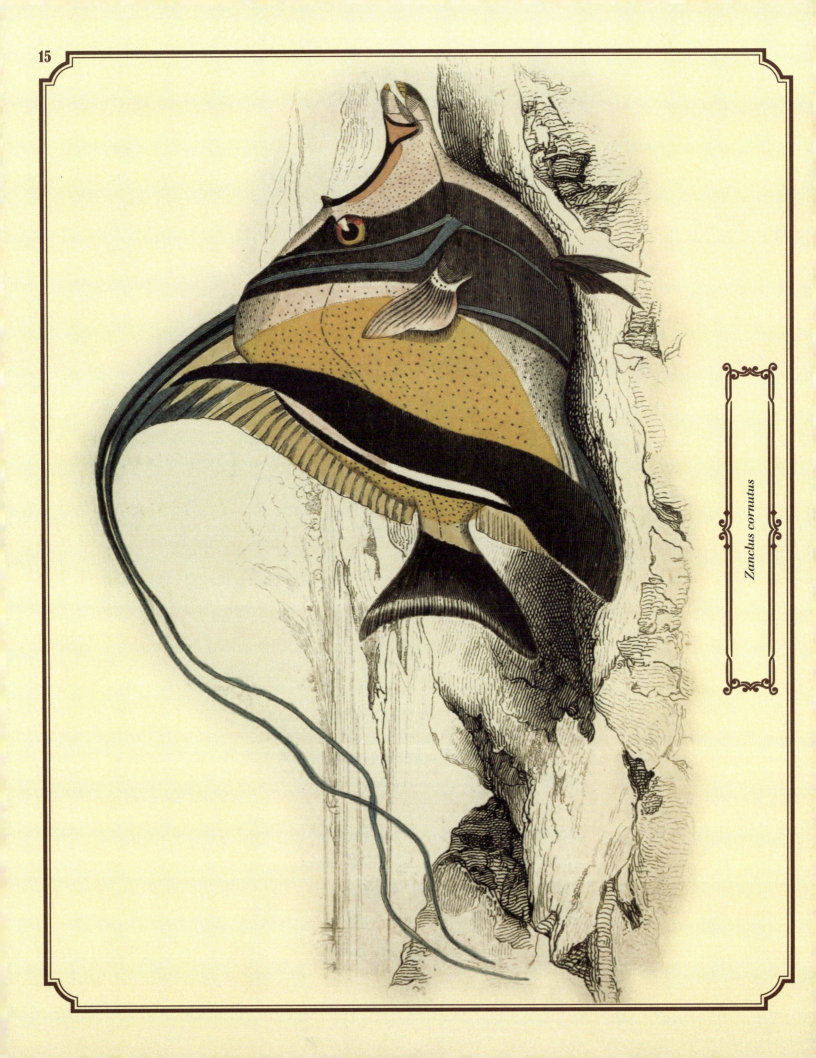

Zanclus cornutus

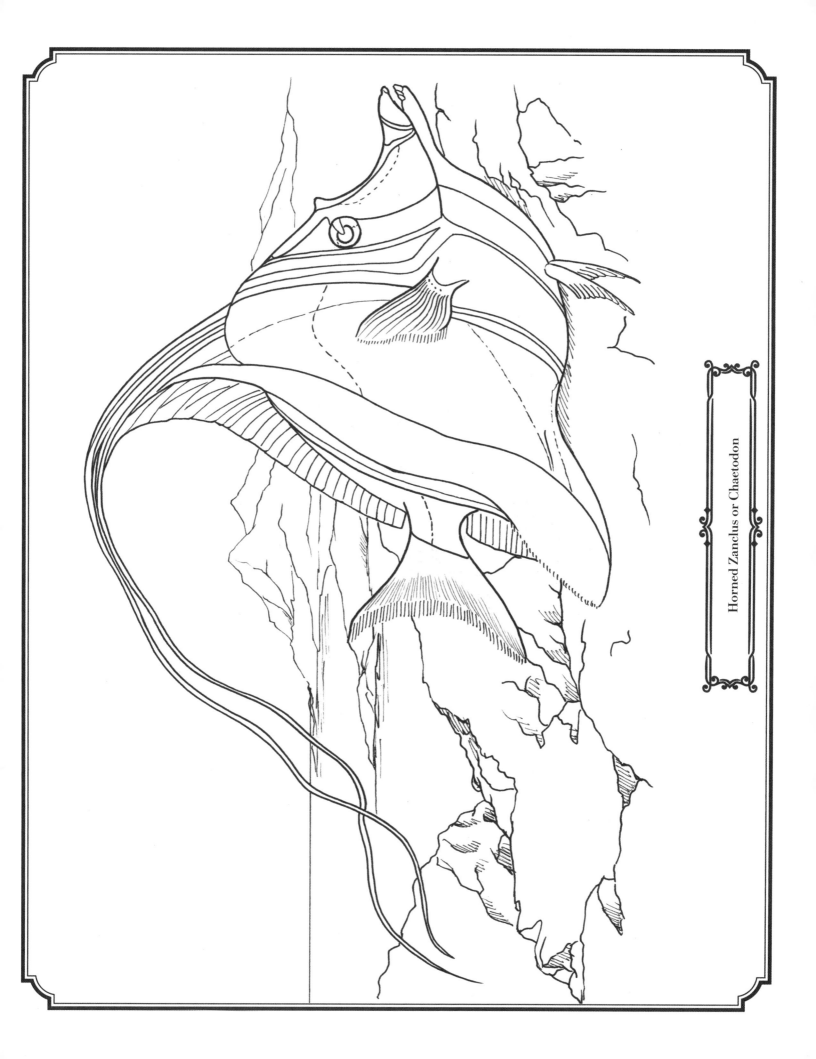

Horned Zanclus or Chaetodon

Argus pteraclis

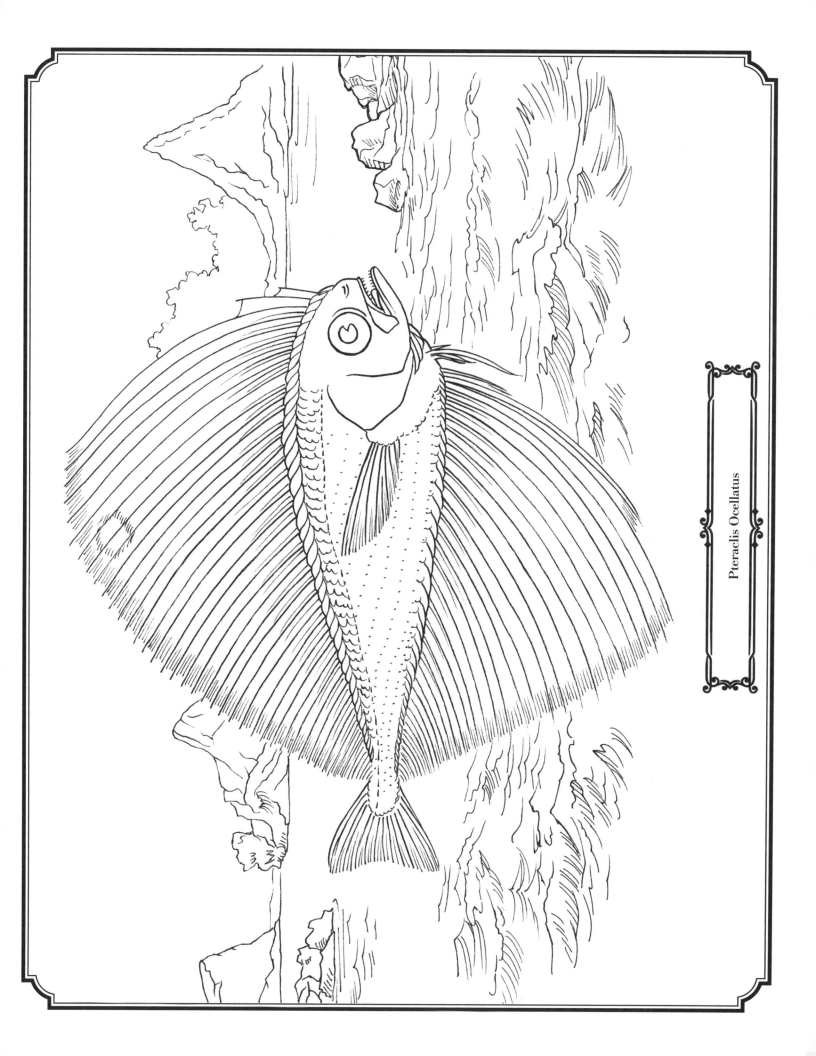

Pteraclis Ocellatus

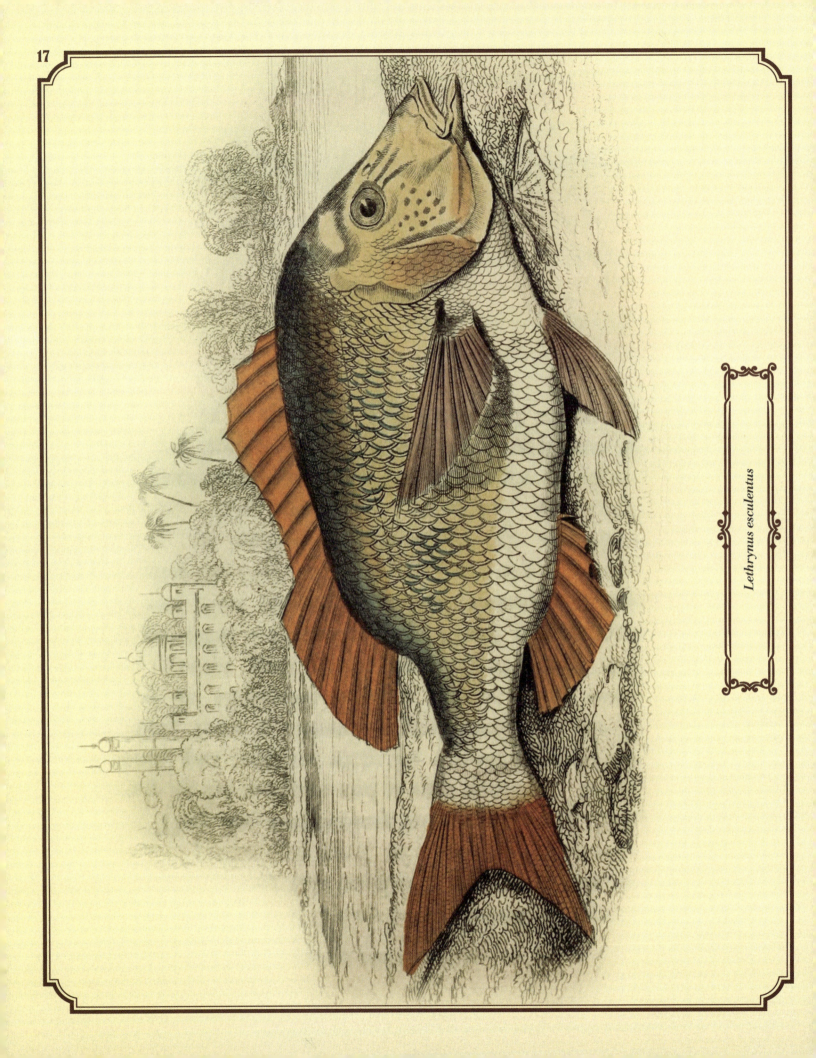
Lethrynus esculentus

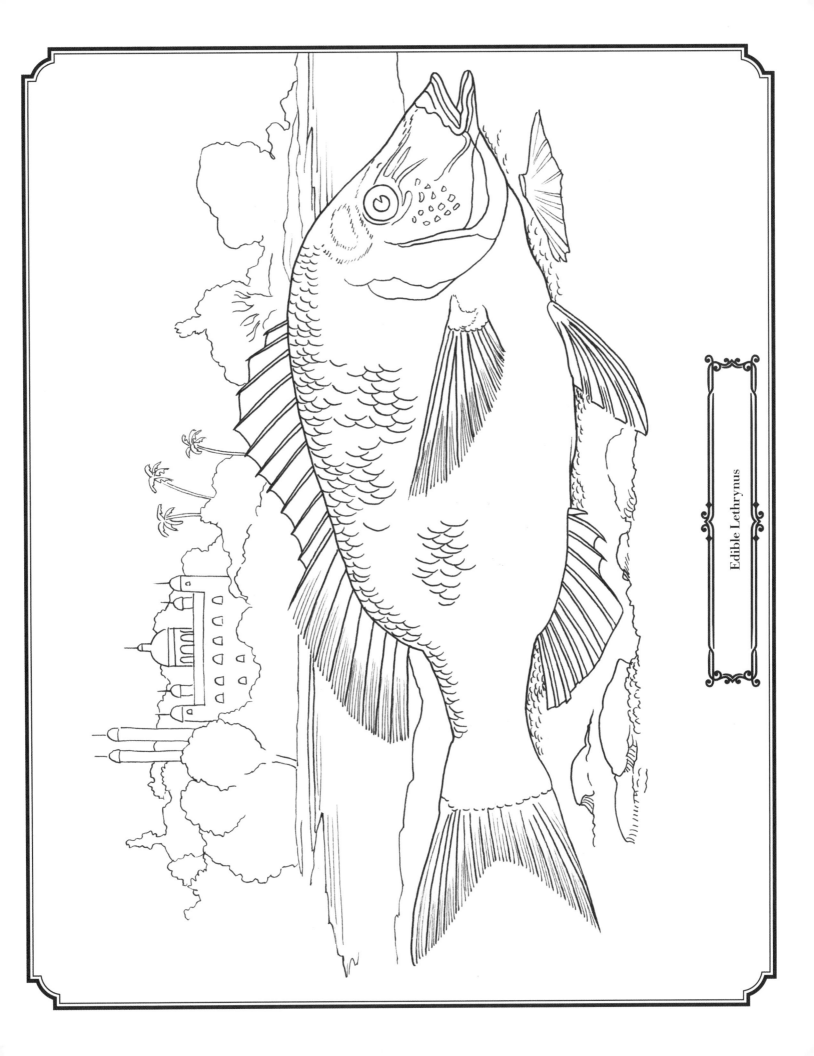

Edible Lethrynus

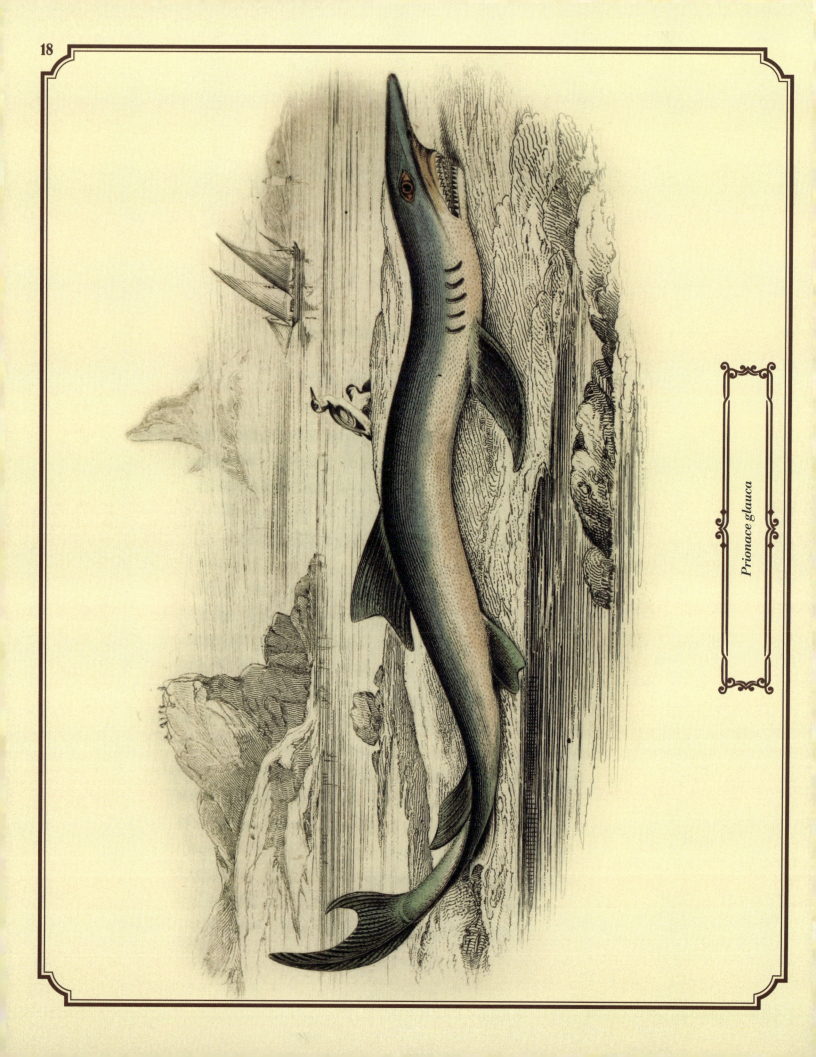

Prionace glauca

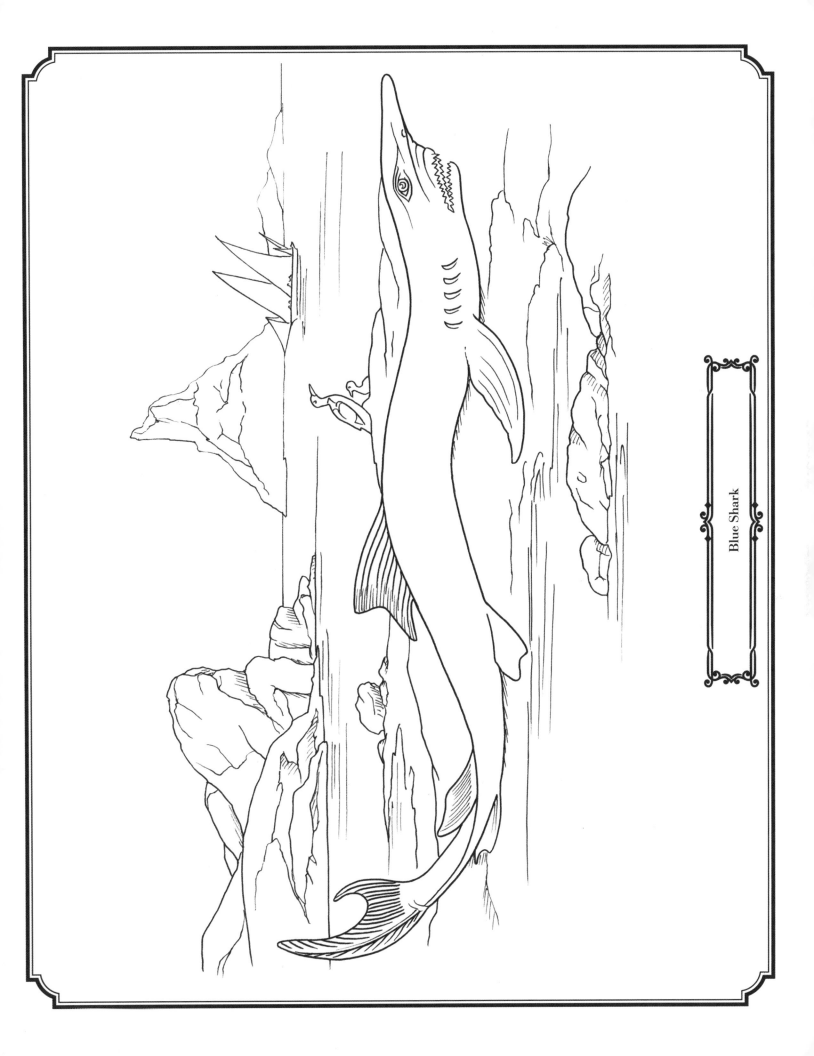
Blue Shark

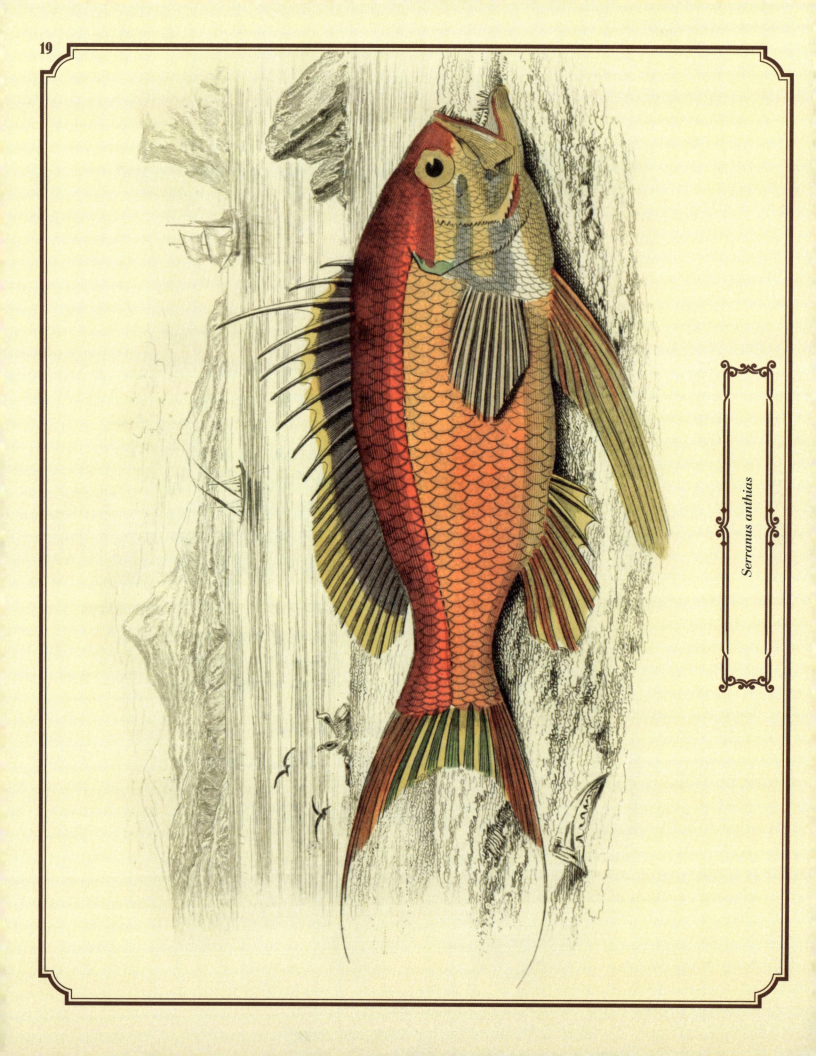

Serranus anthias

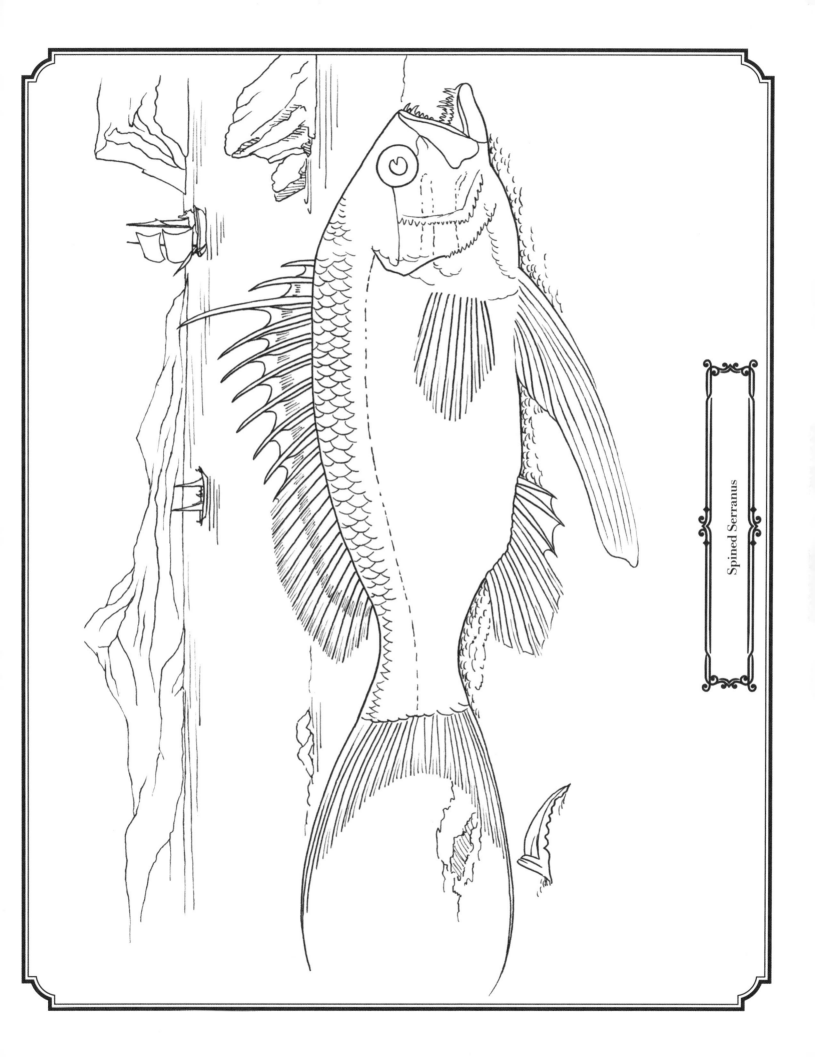

Spined Serranus

Monocentris cornutus

Armed Monocentris

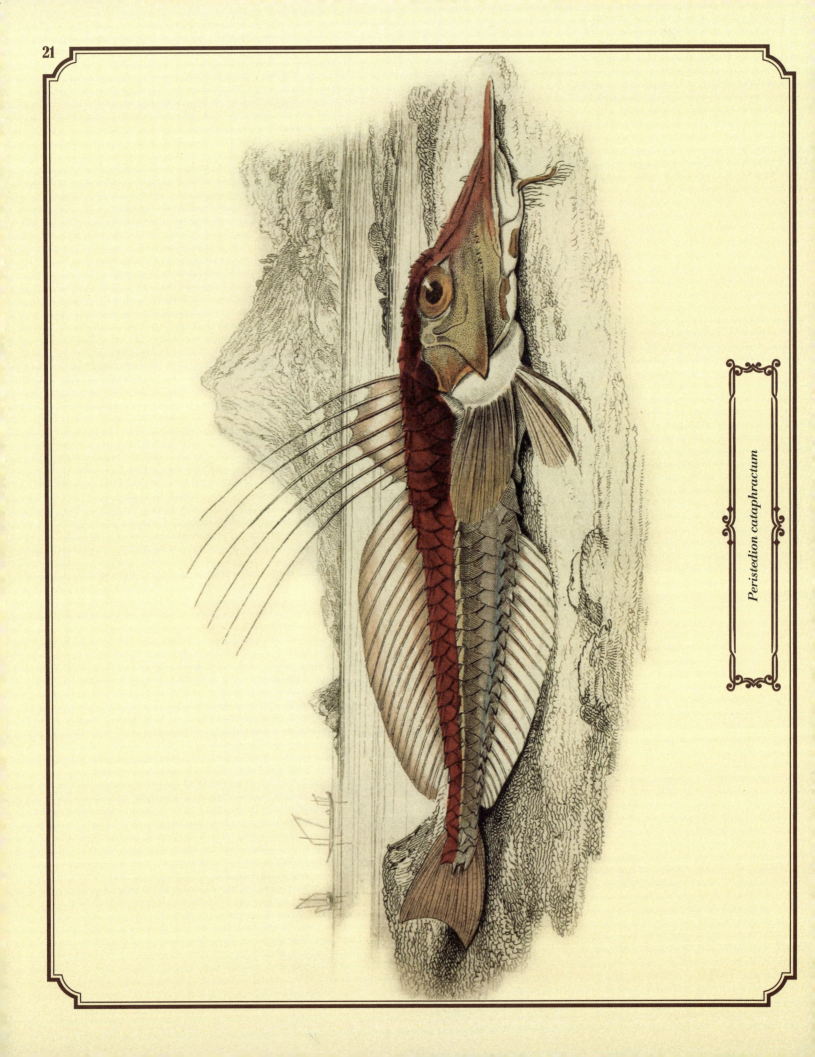

Peristedion cataphractum

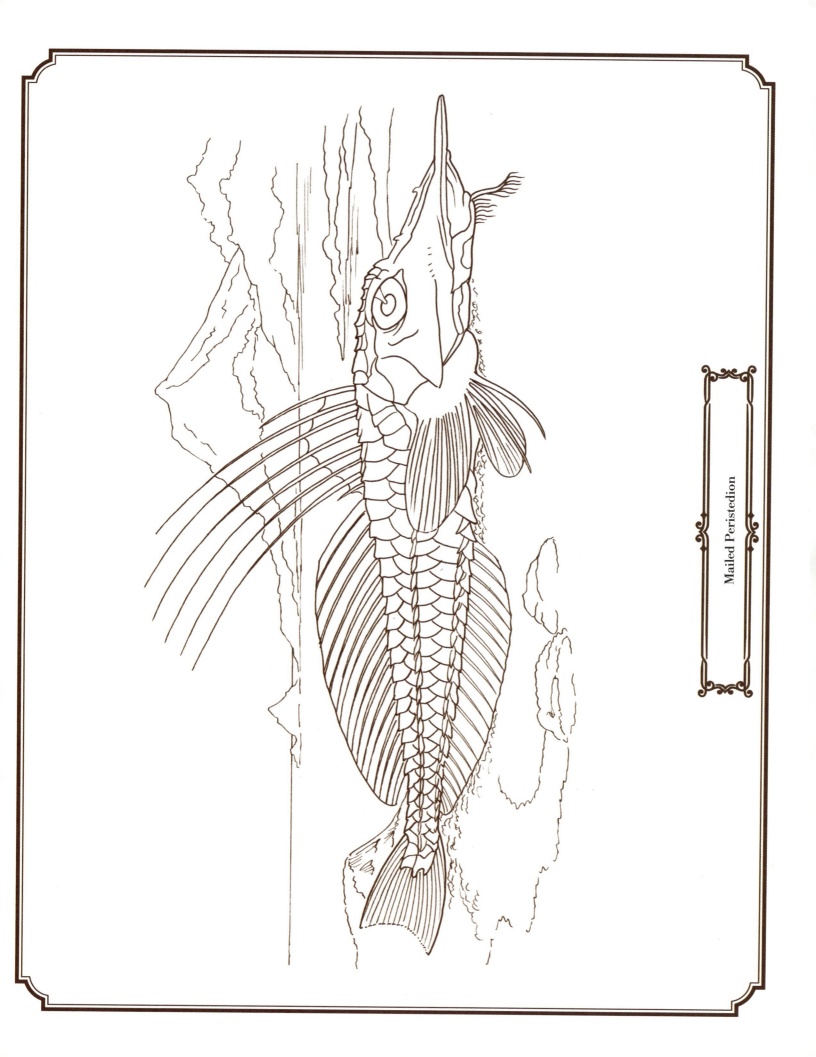

Mailed Peristedion

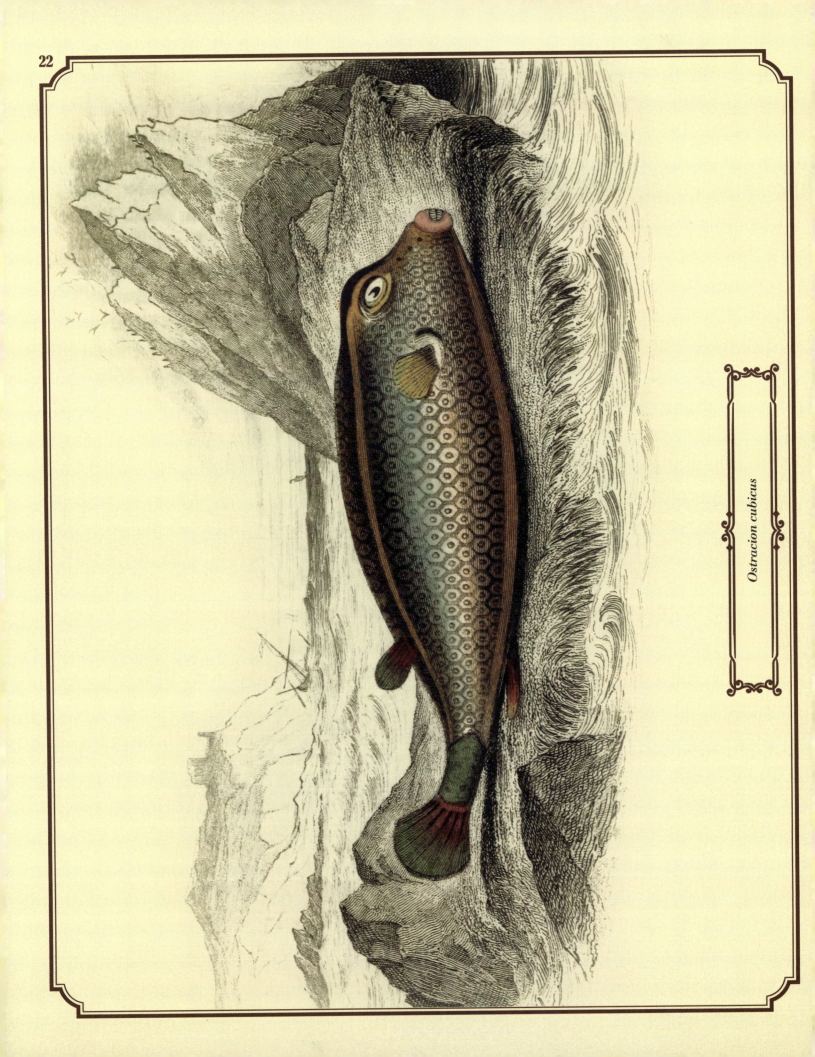

Ostracion cubicus

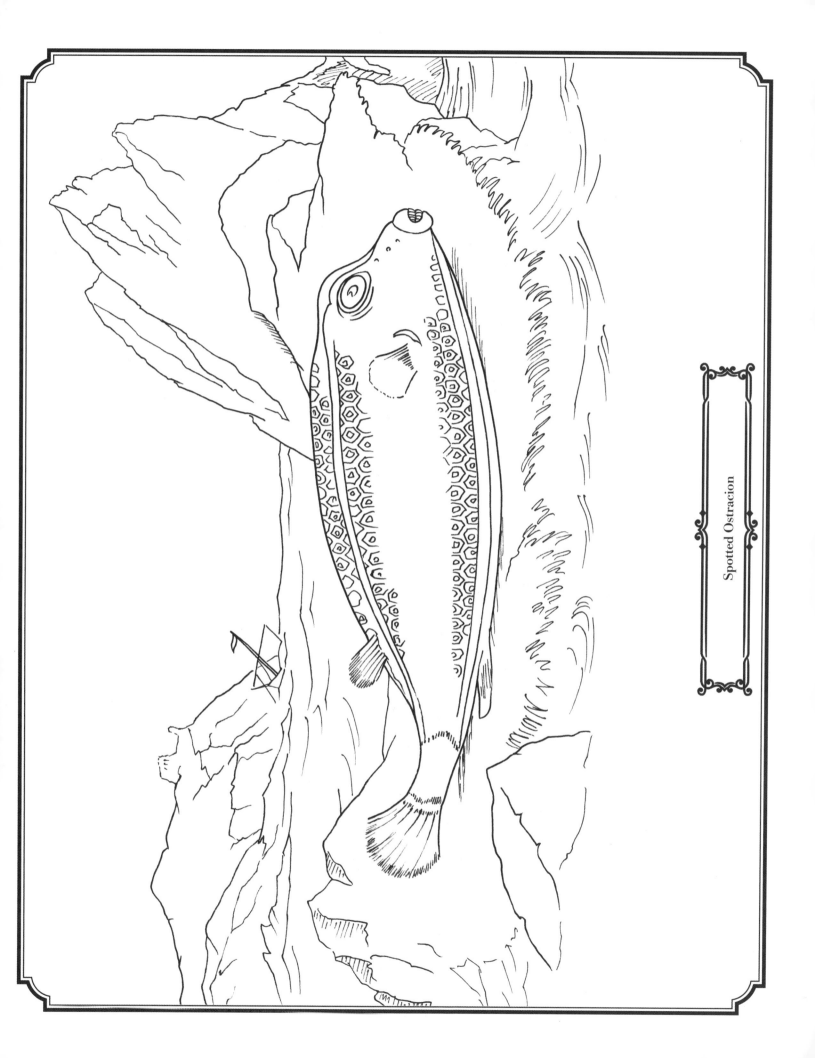
Spotted Ostracion

23

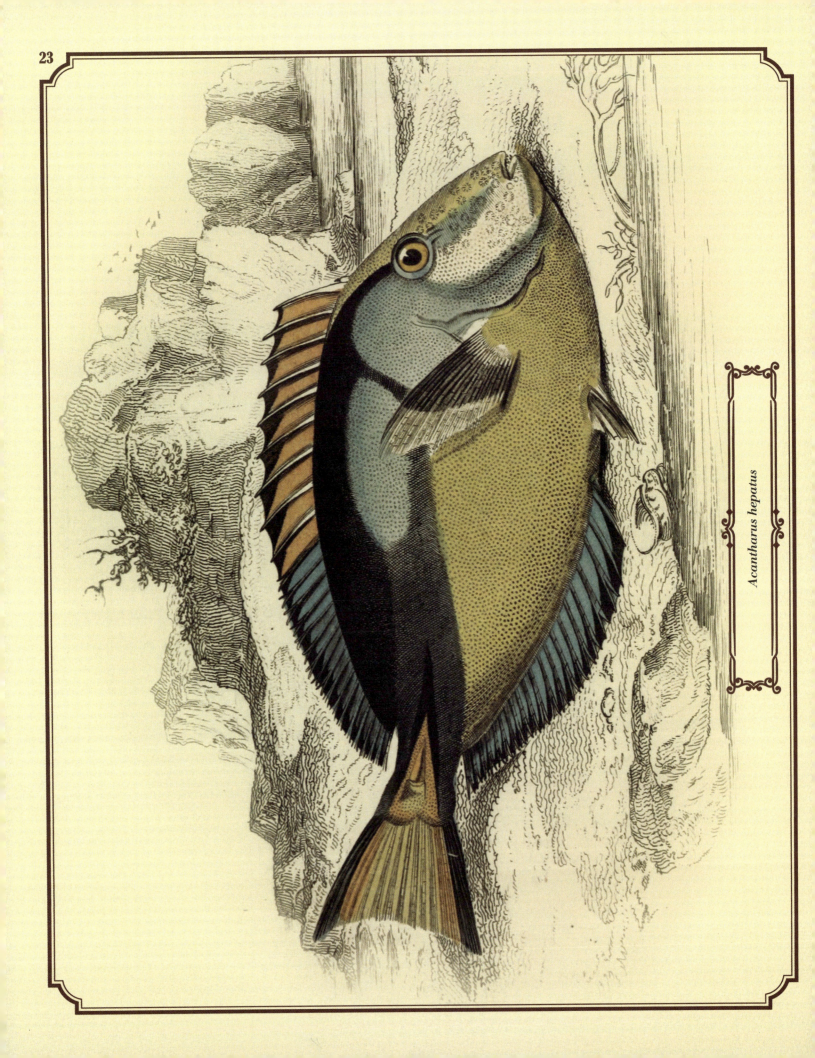

Acantharus hepatus

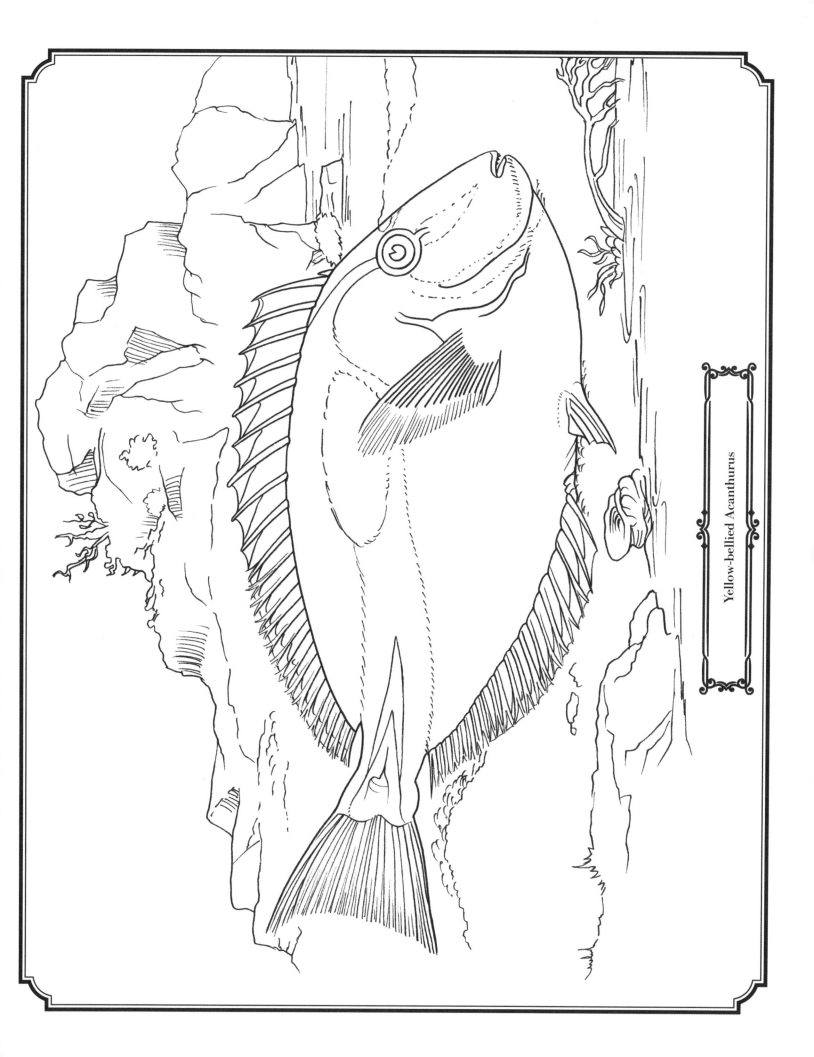

Yellow-bellied Acanthurus

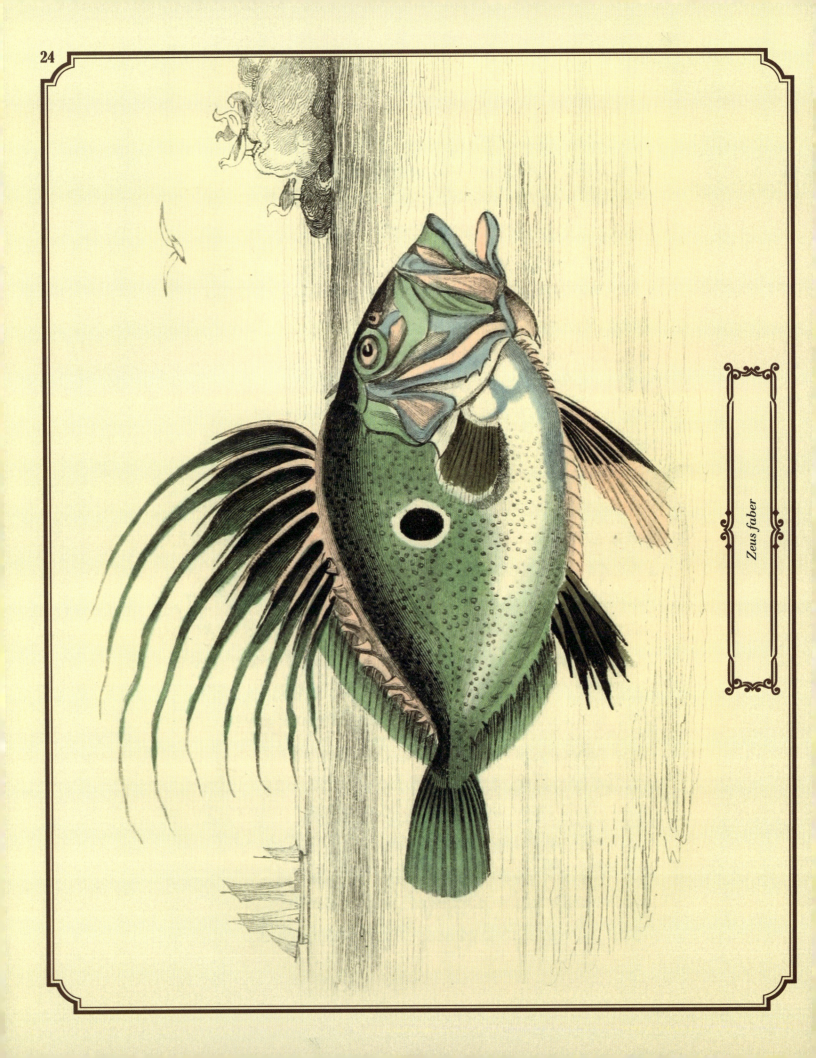

Zeus faber

John Dory

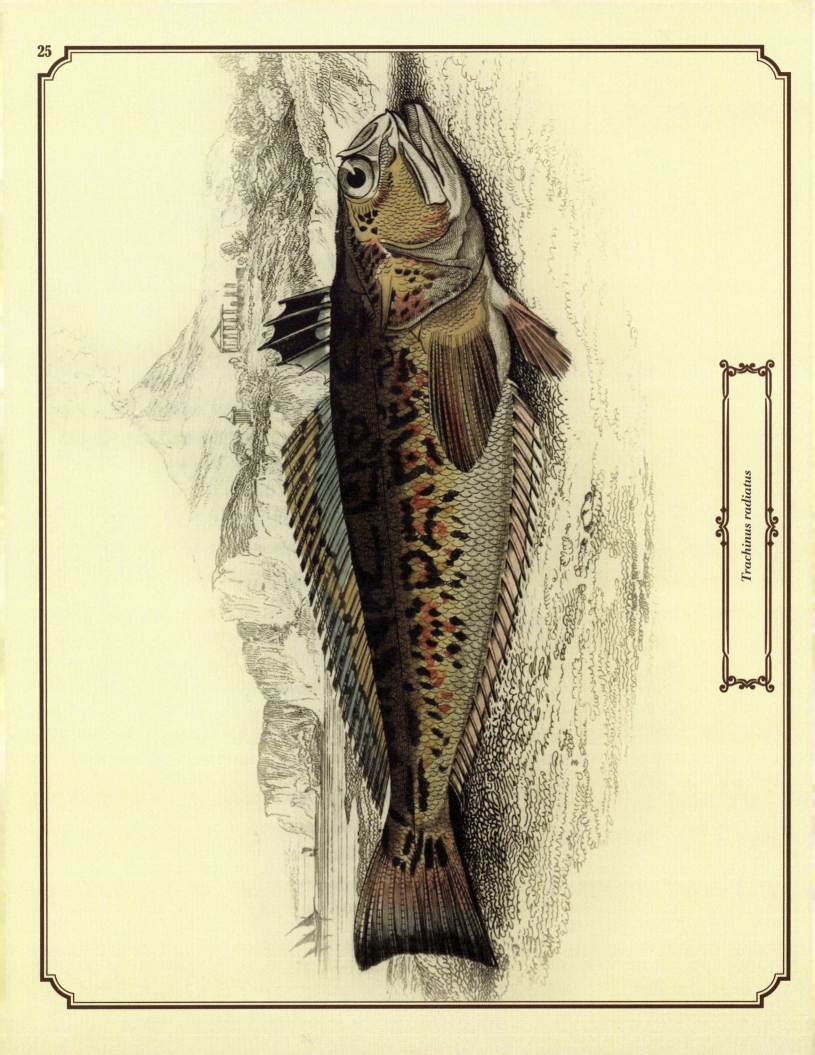

Trachinus radiatus

Radiated Weaver

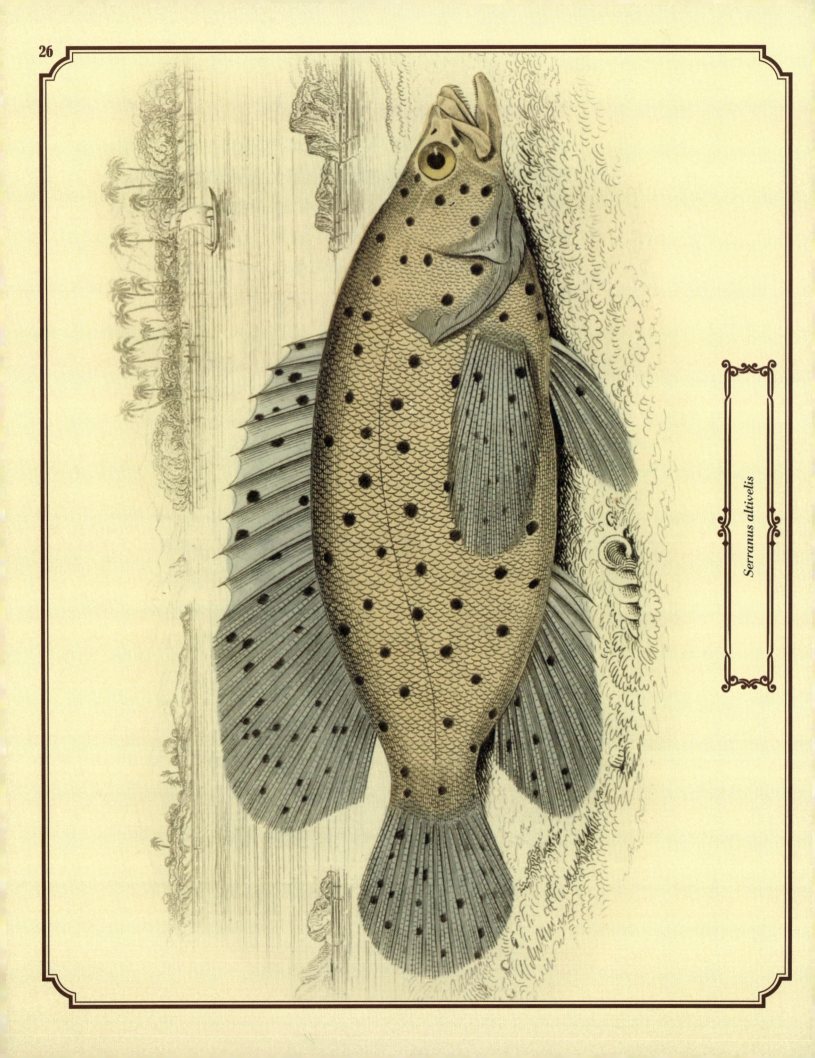

Serranus altivelis

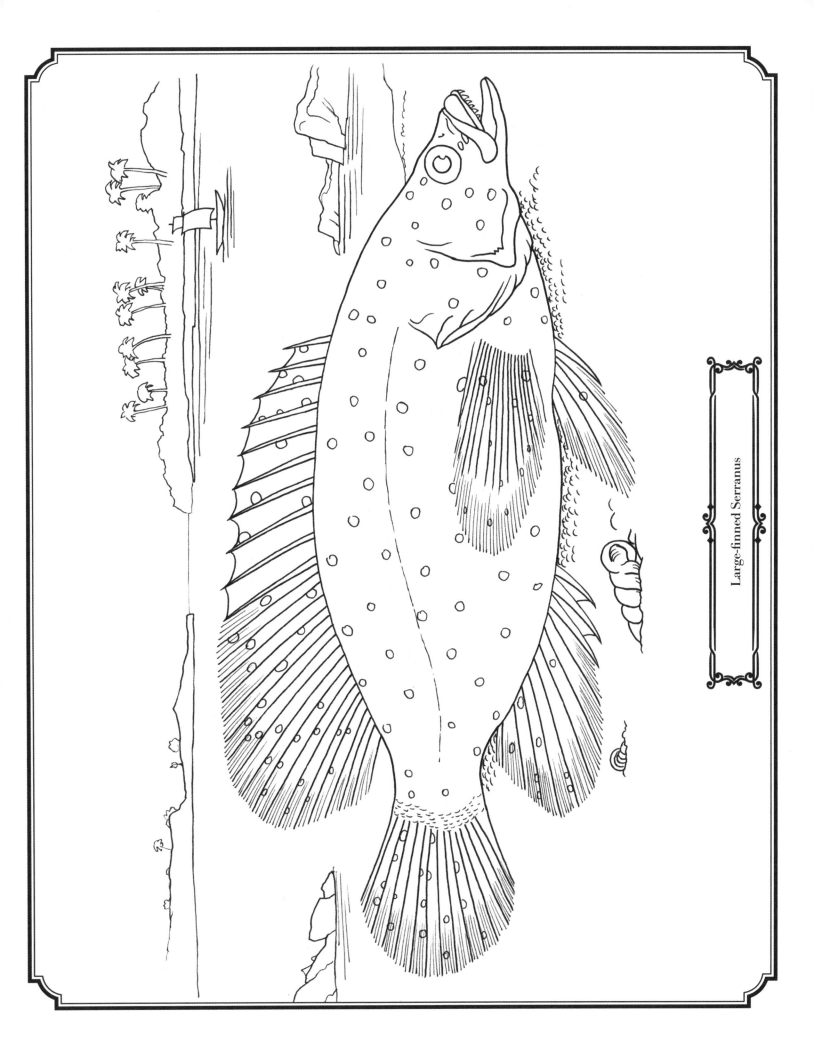

Large-finned Serranus

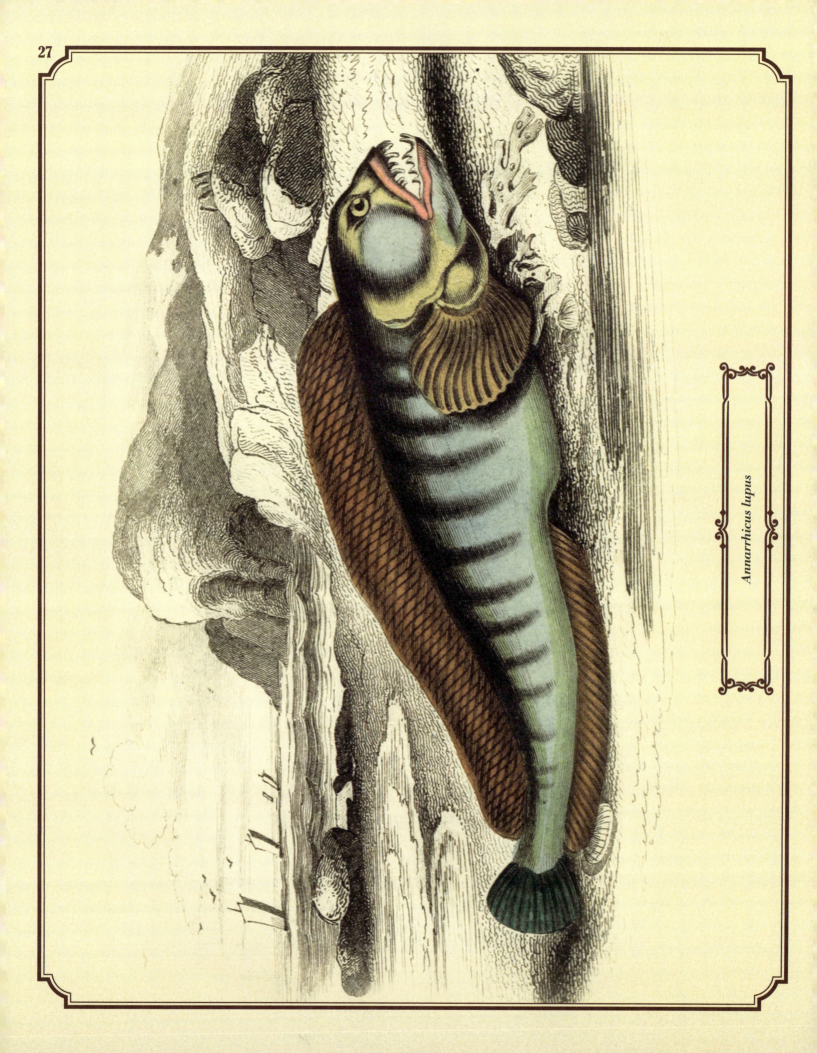

Annarrhicus lupus

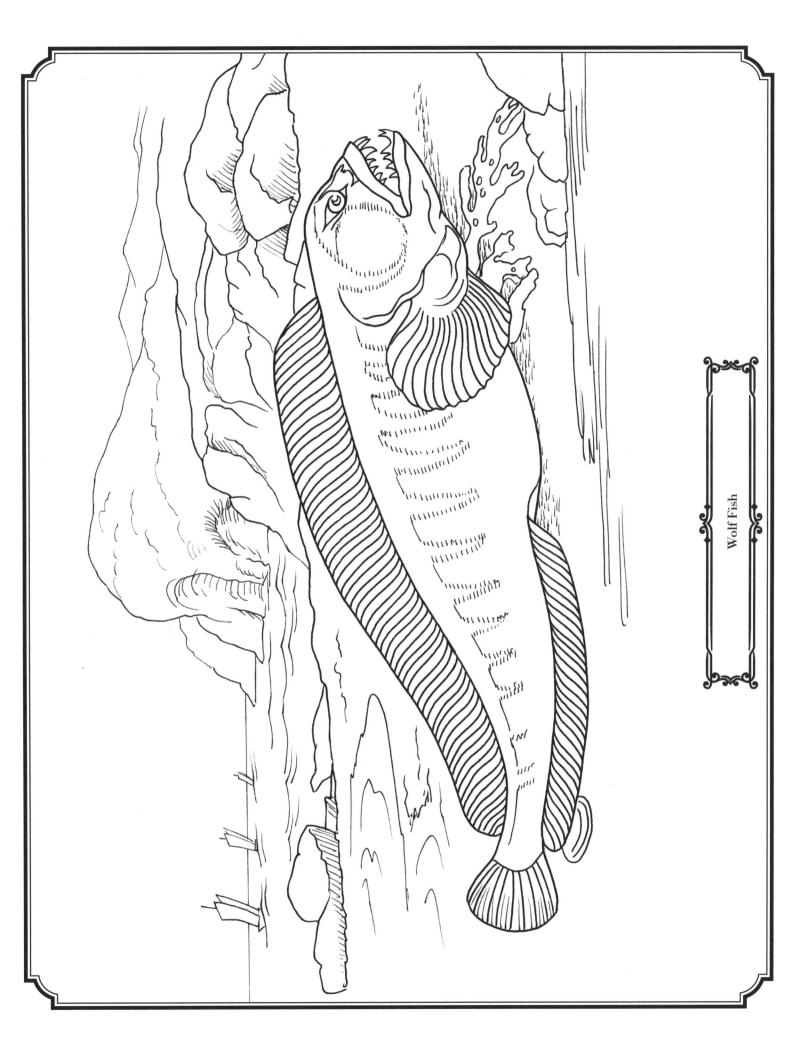

Wolf Fish

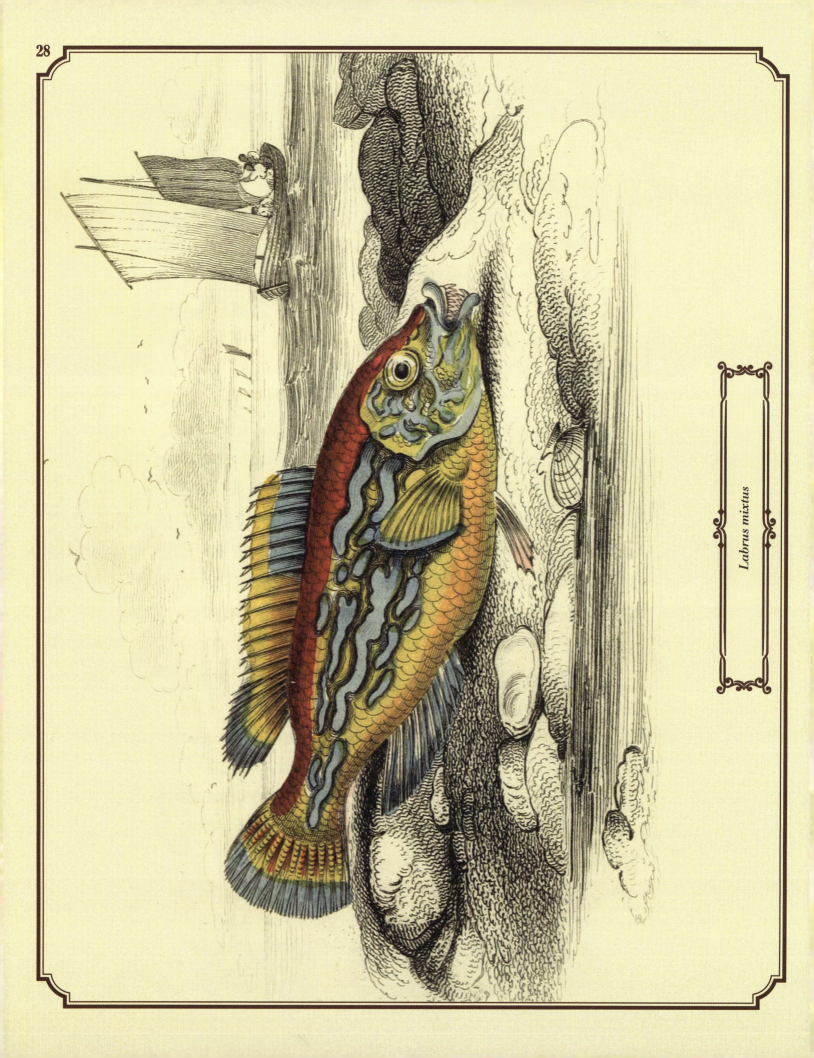
Labrus mixtus

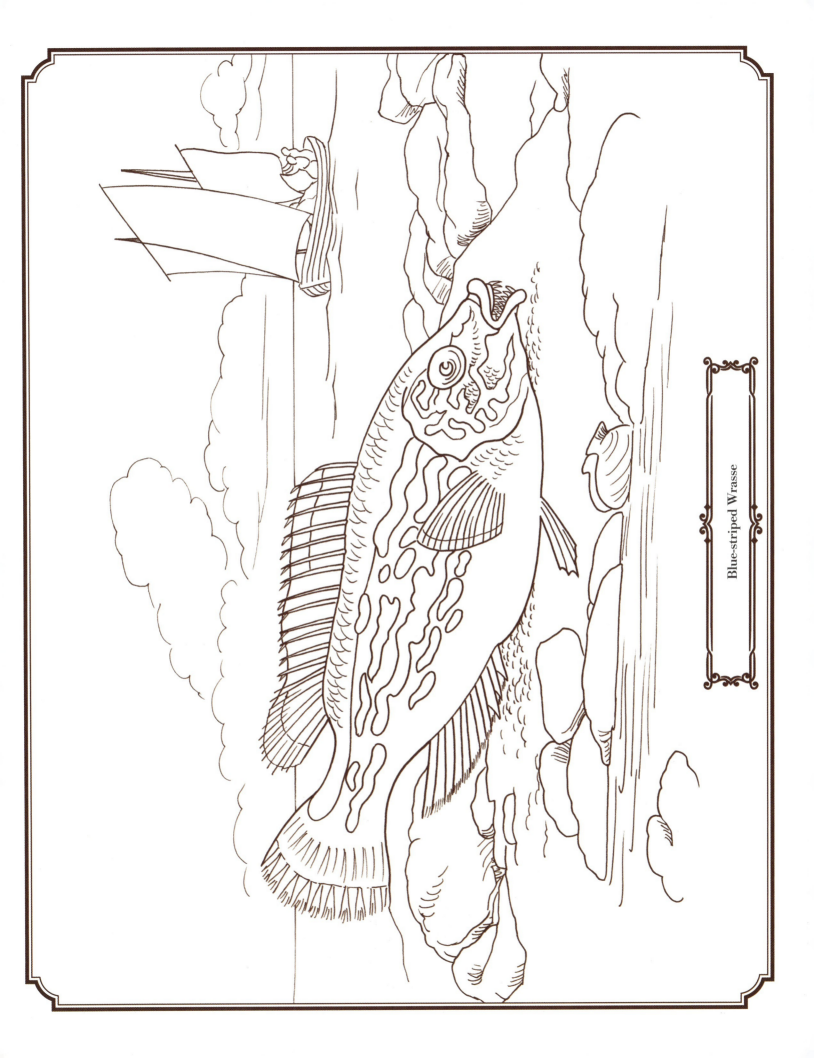
Blue-striped Wrasse

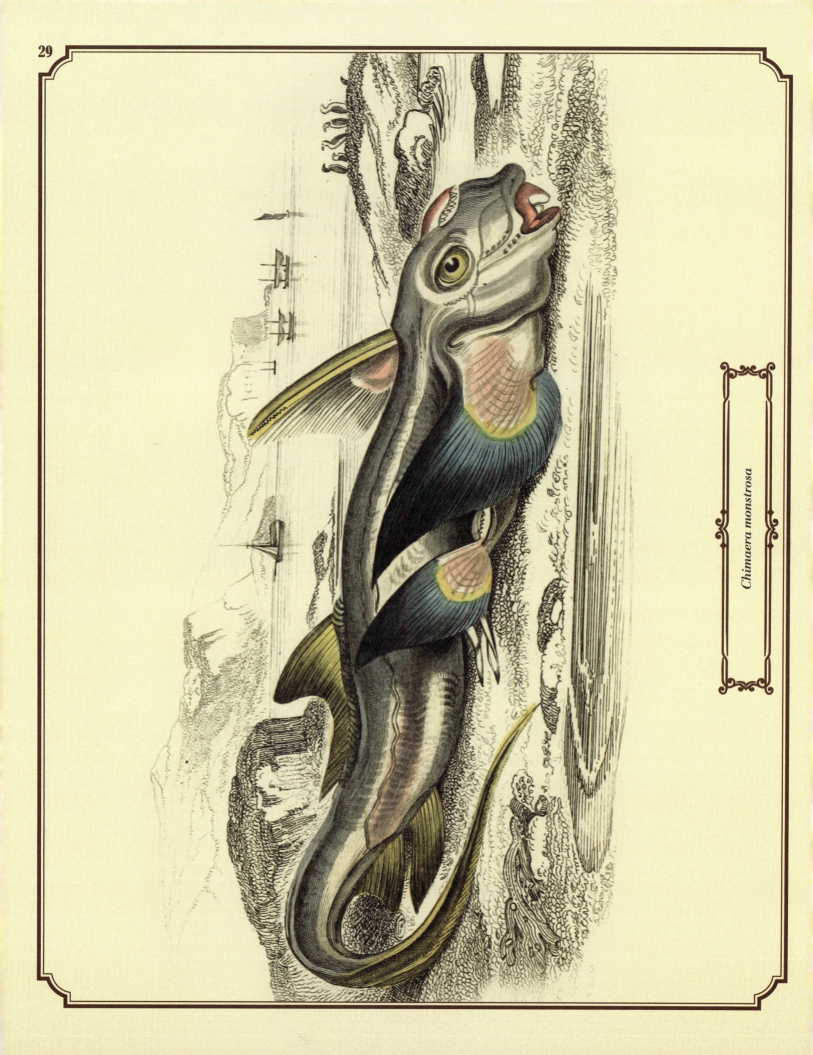

Chimaera monstrosa

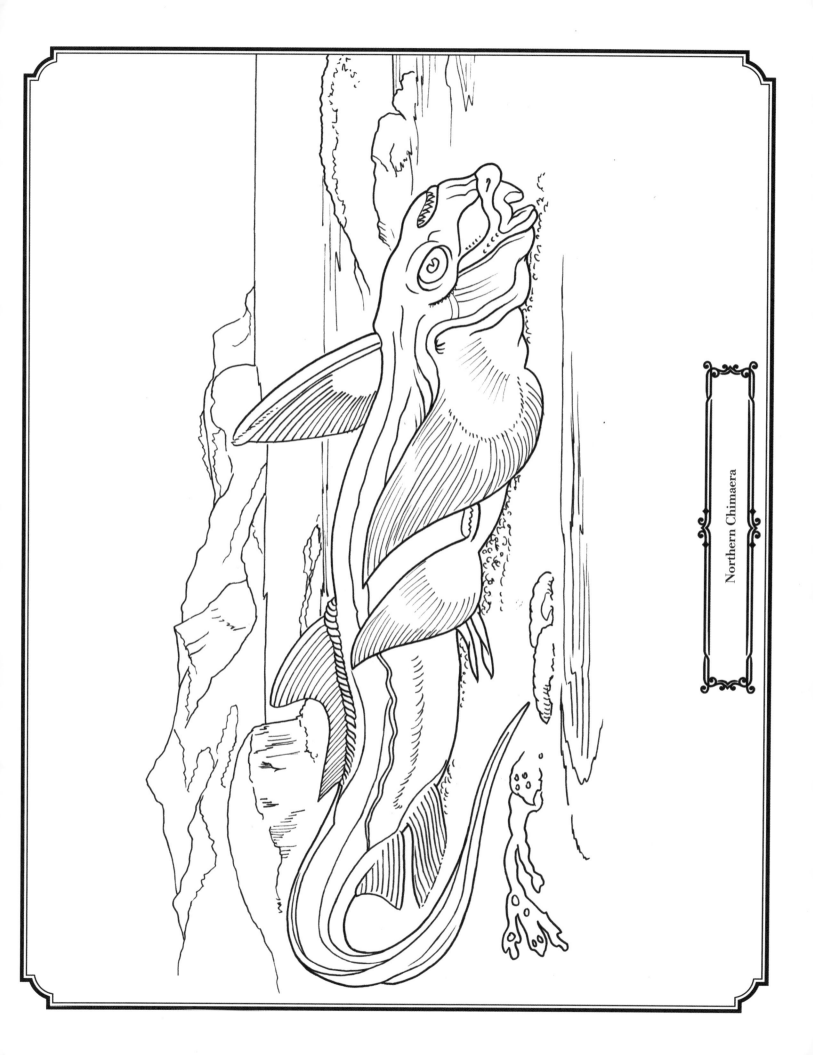

Northern Chimaera

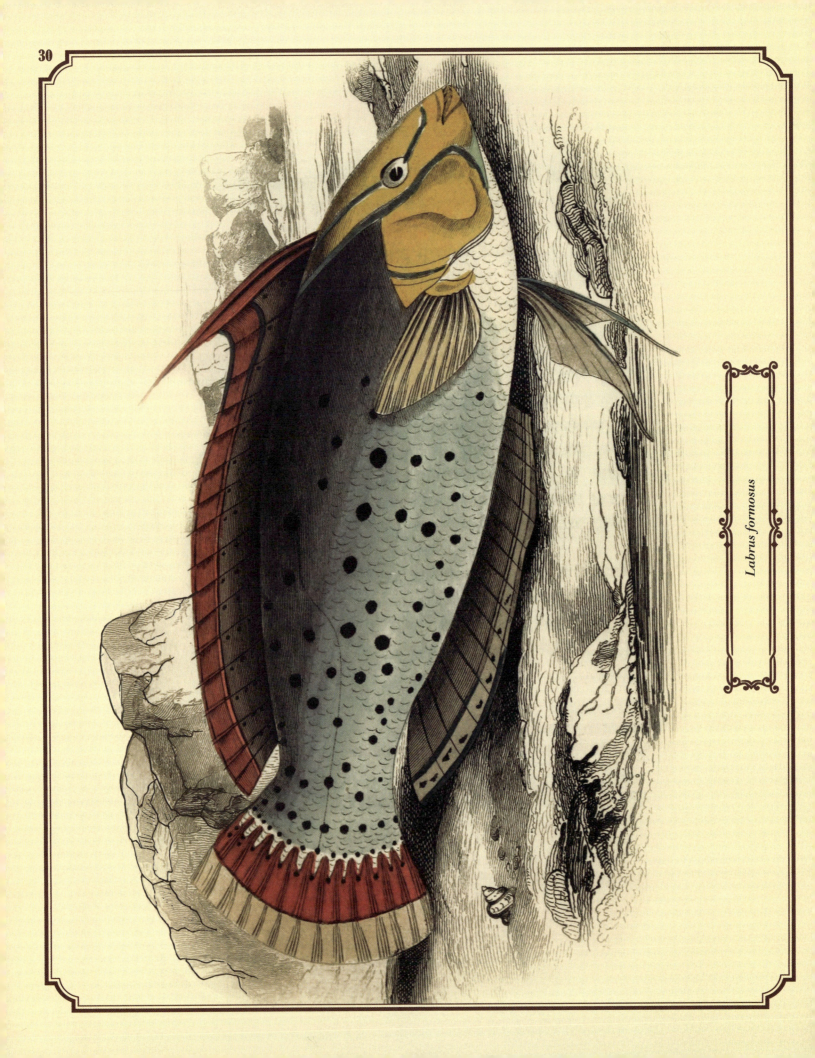
Labrus formosus

Painted Labrus

Cychla rubro-ocellata

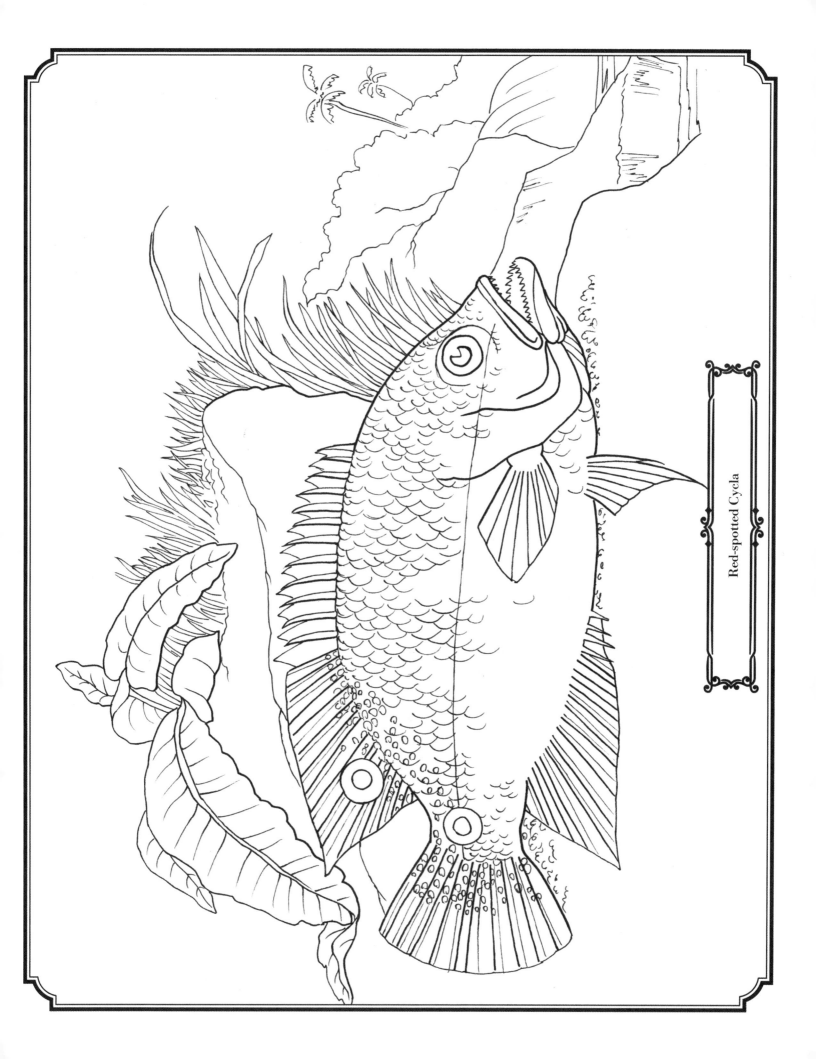
Red-spotted Cycla

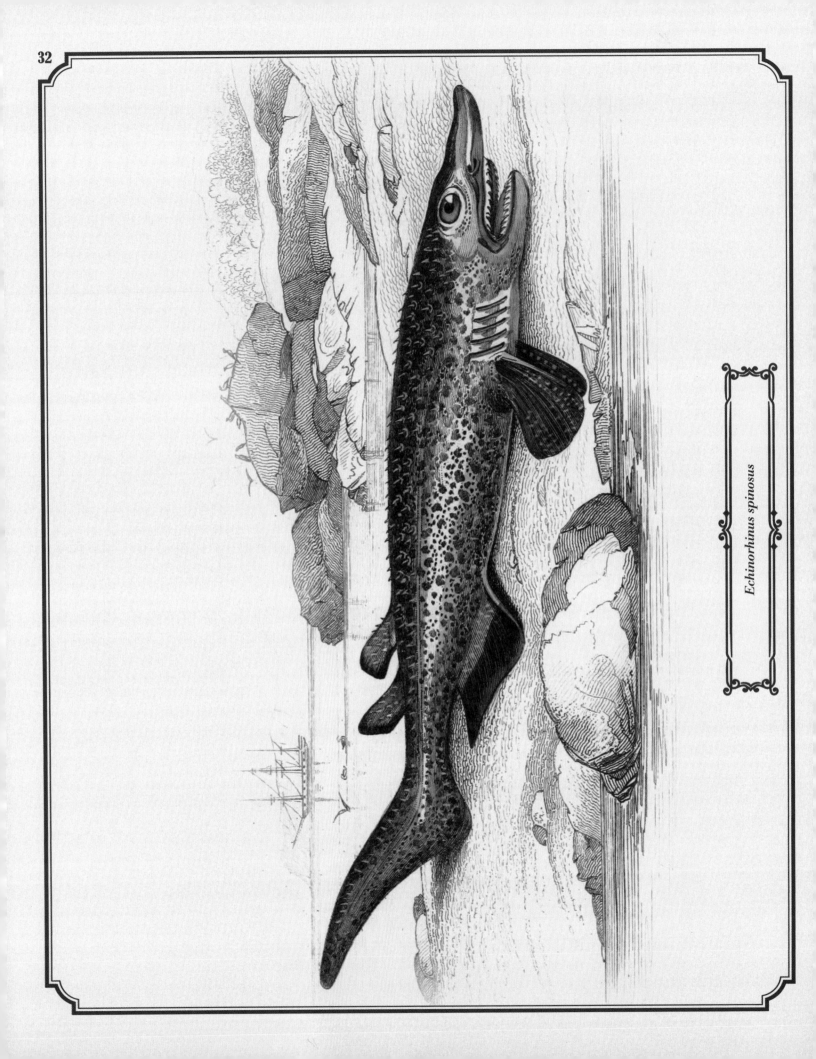

Echinorhinus spinosus

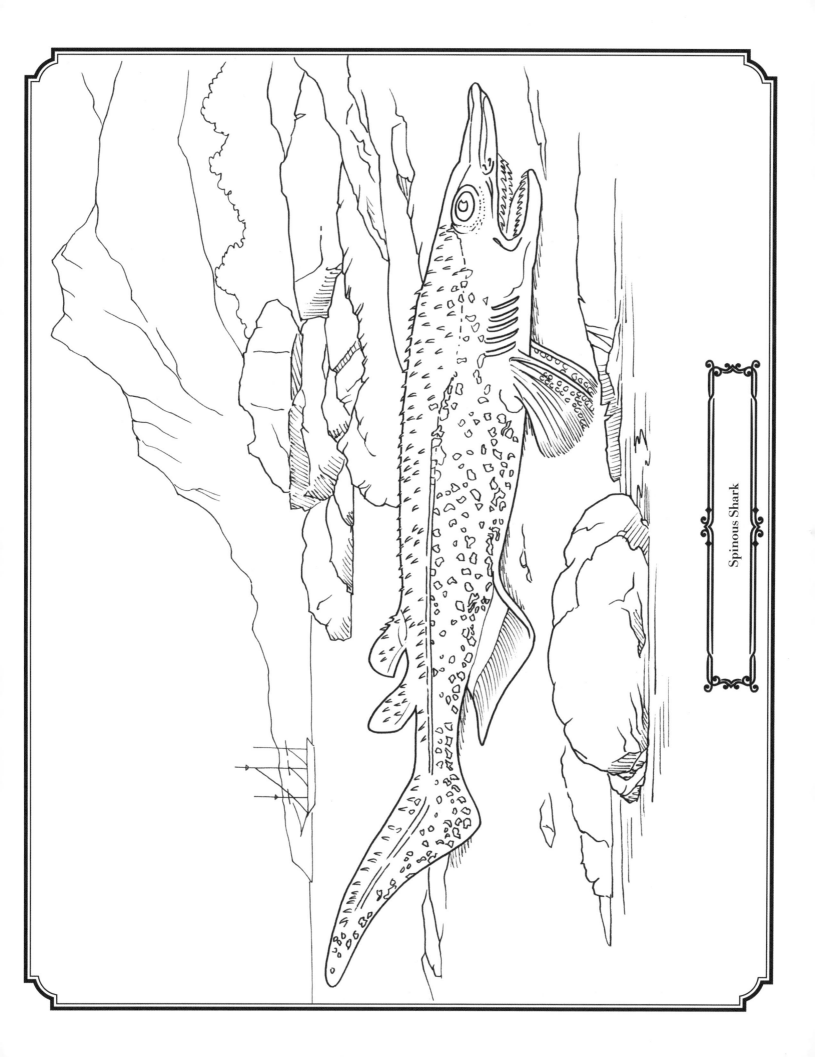

Spinous Shark

Huro nigricanus

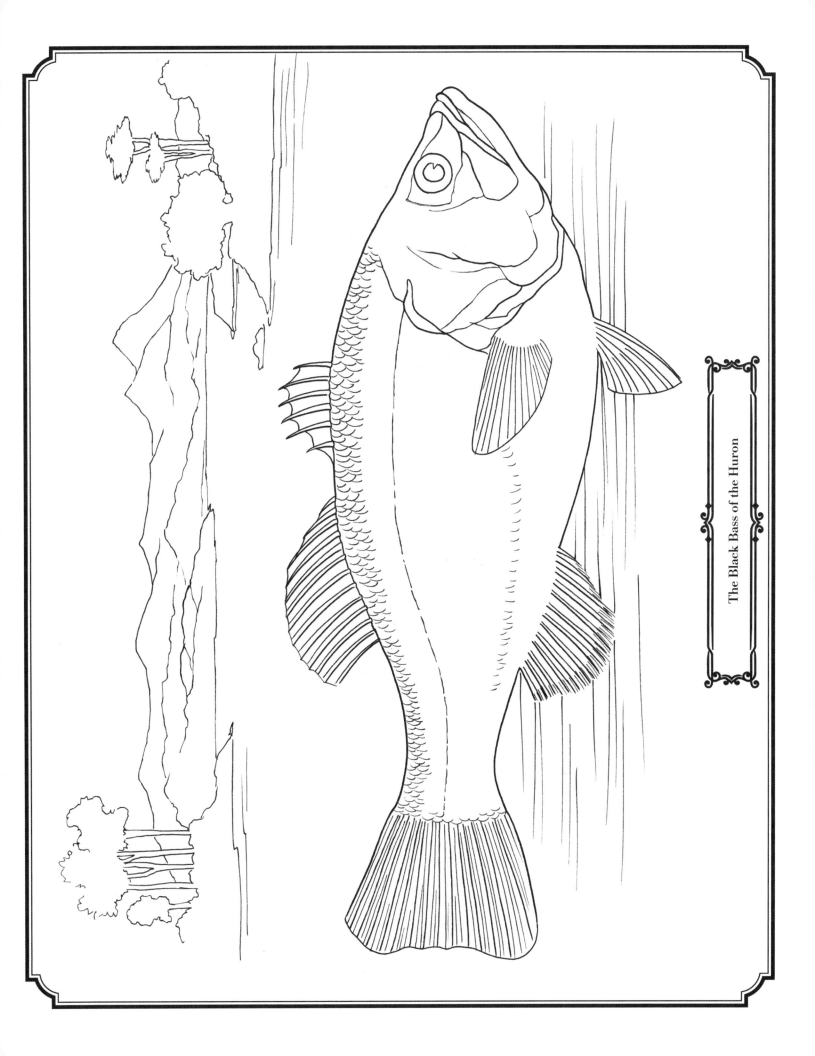
The Black Bass of the Huron

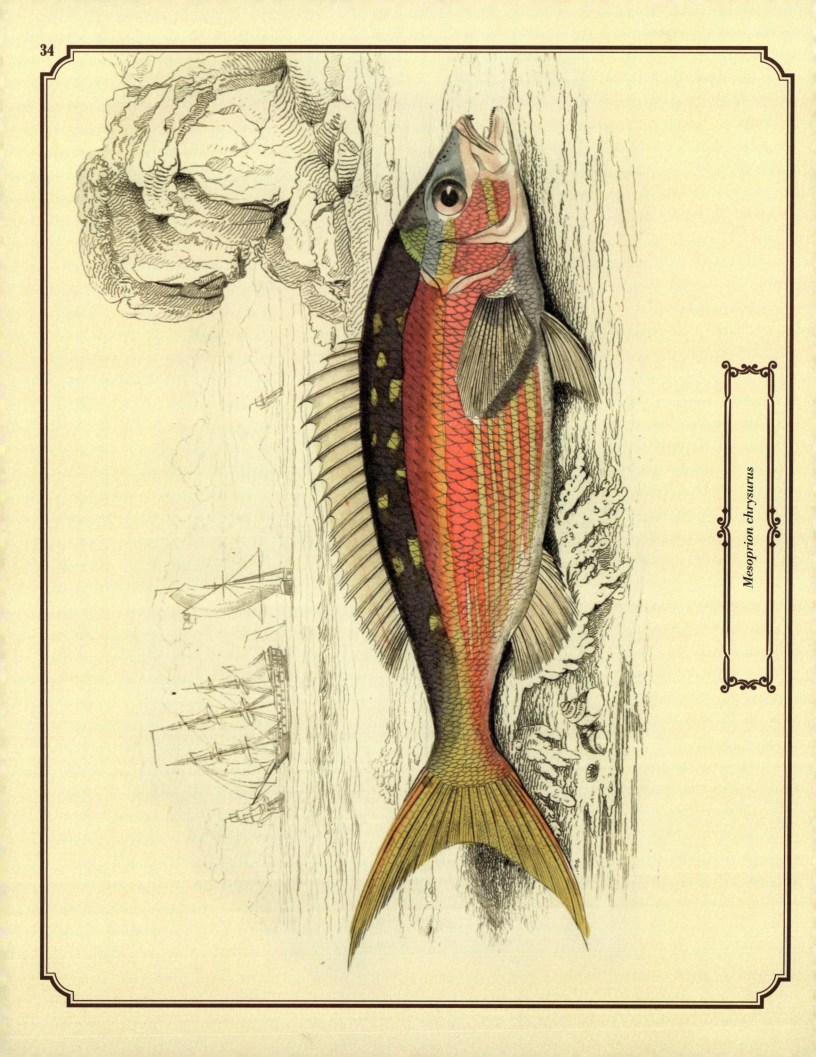

Mesoprion chrysurus

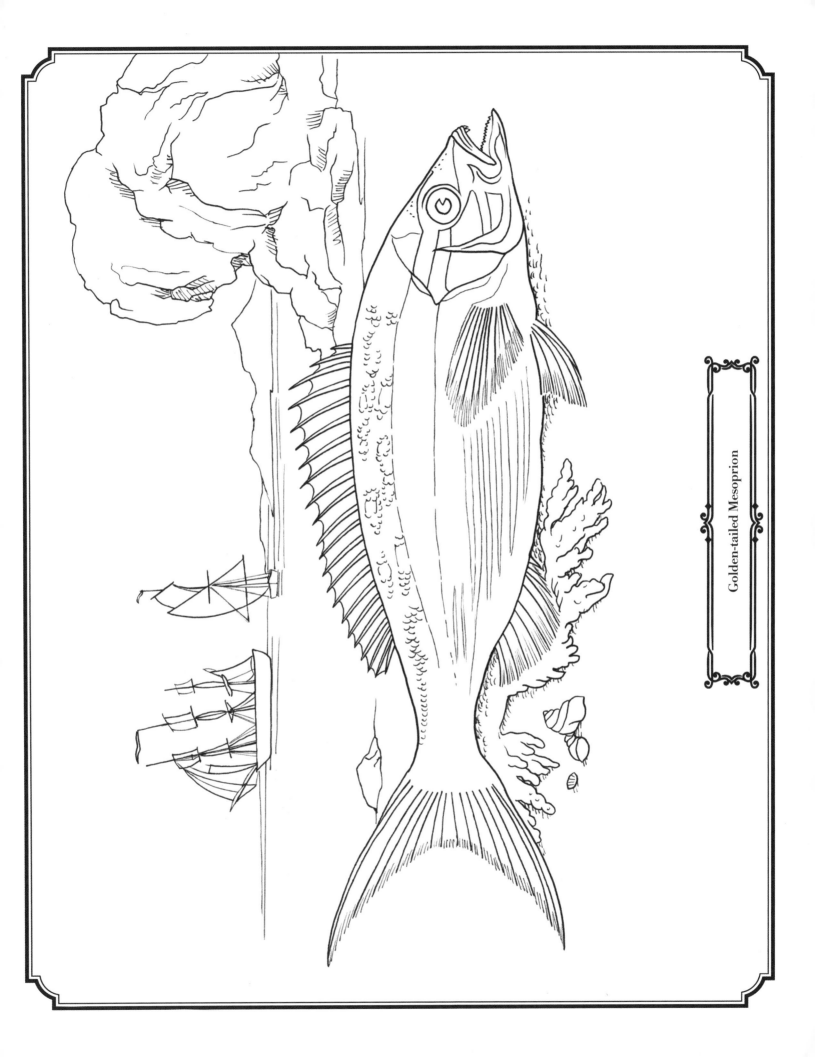
Golden-tailed Mesoprion

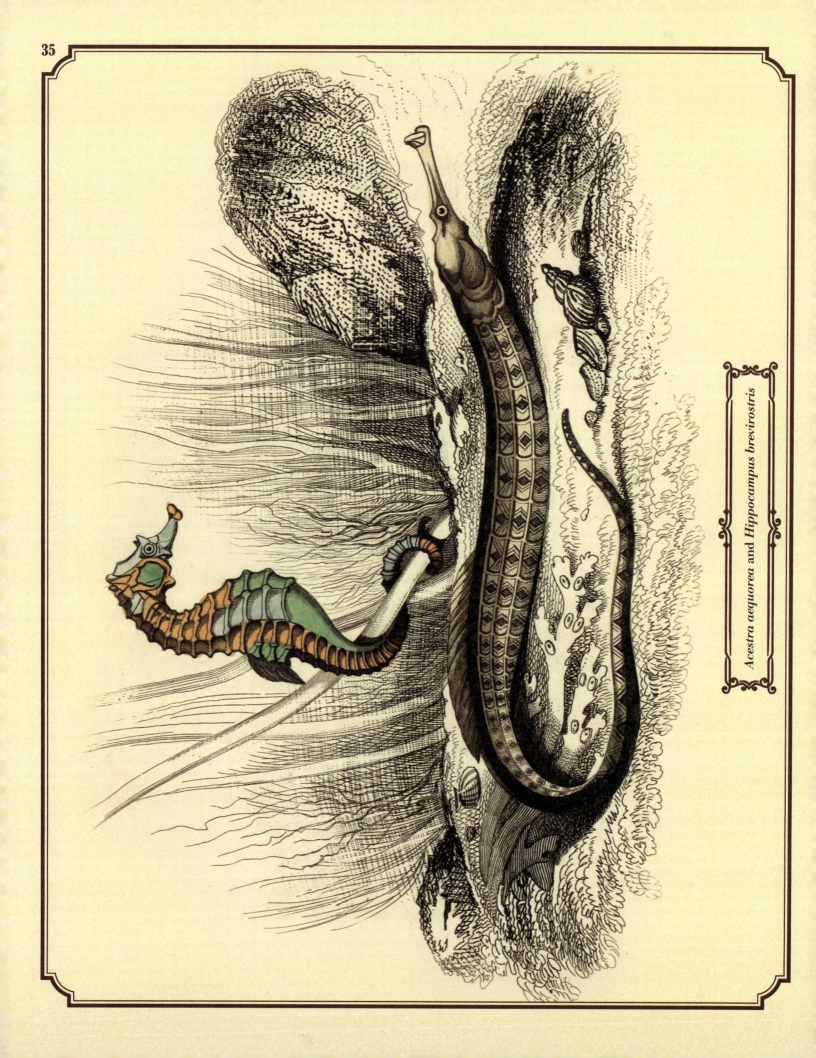

Acestra aequorea and *Hippocampus brevirostris*

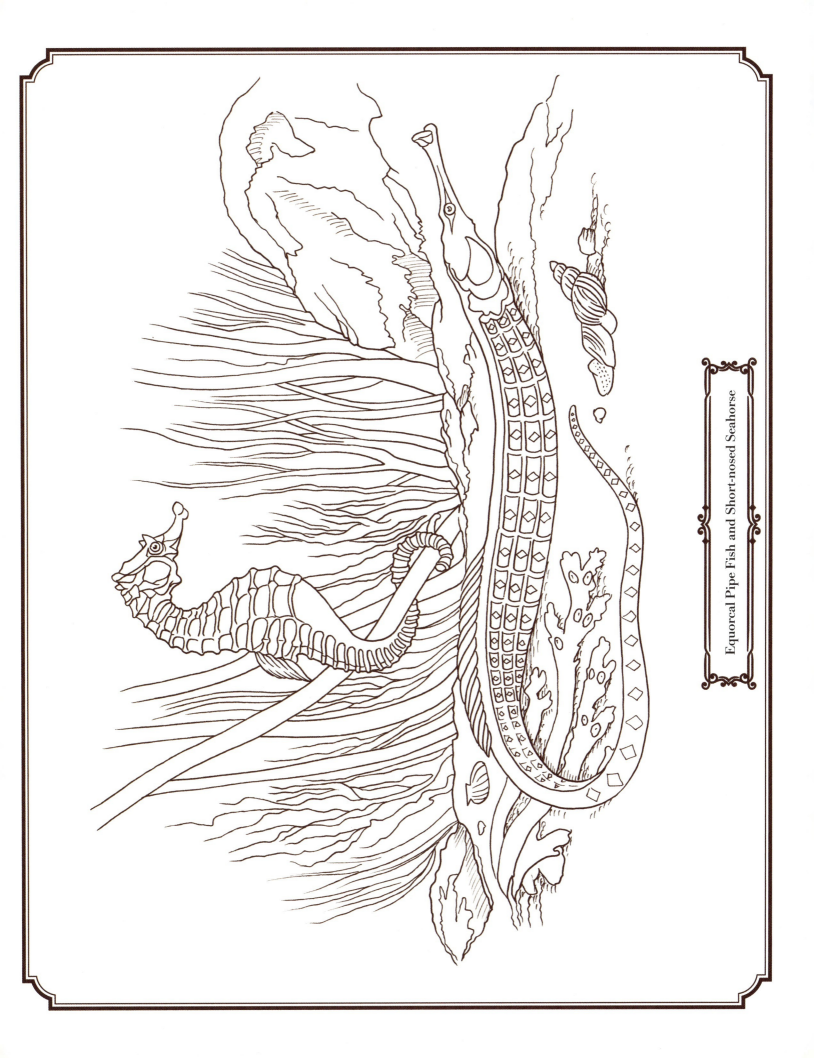

Equorcal Pipe Fish and Short-nosed Seahorse

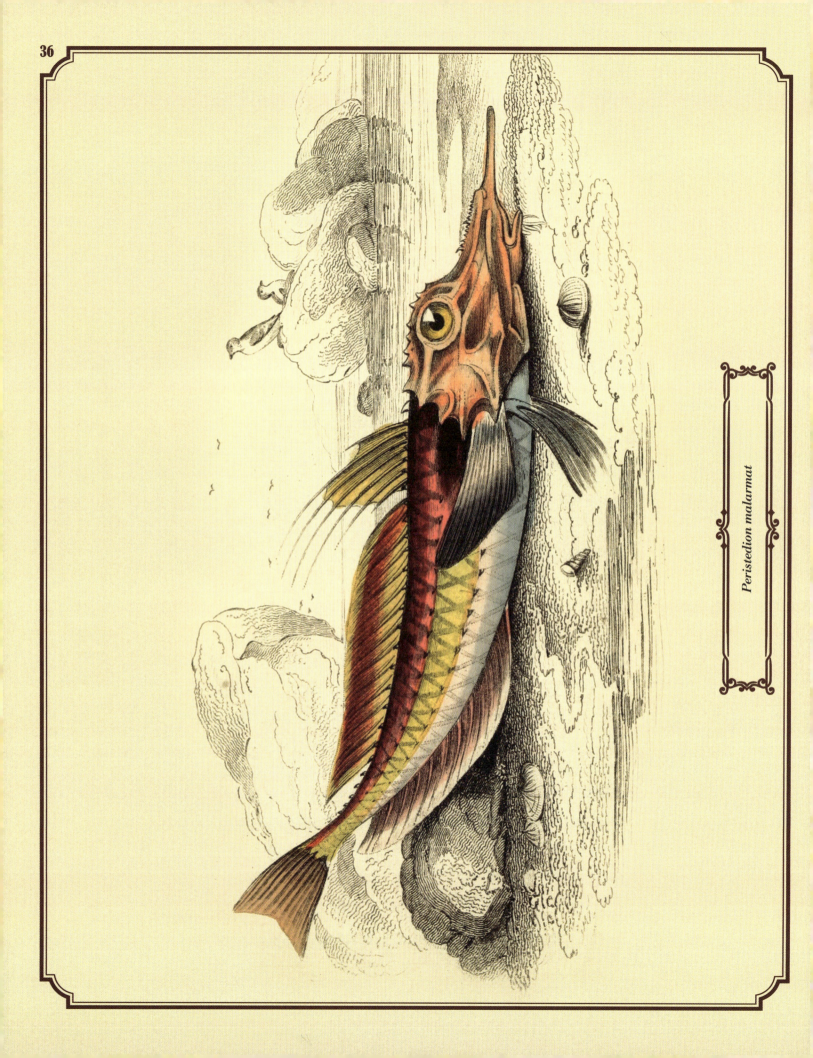
Peristedion malarmat

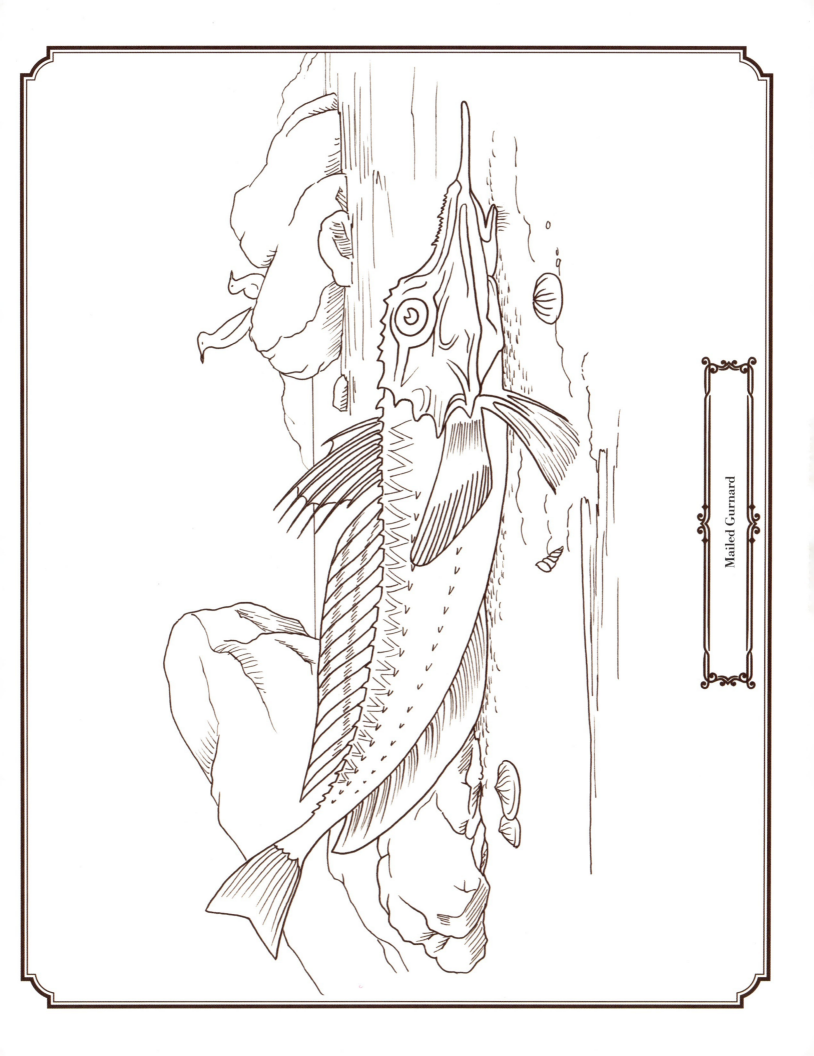

Mailed Gurnard

Acerina vulgaris

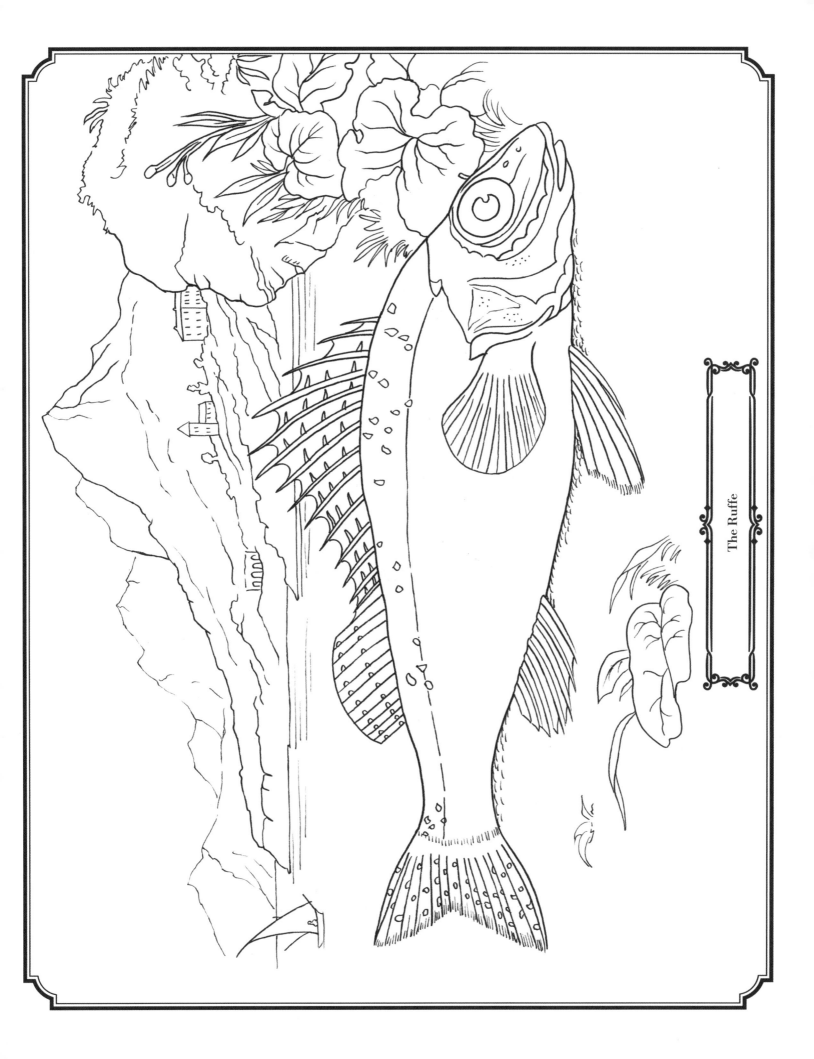

The Ruffe

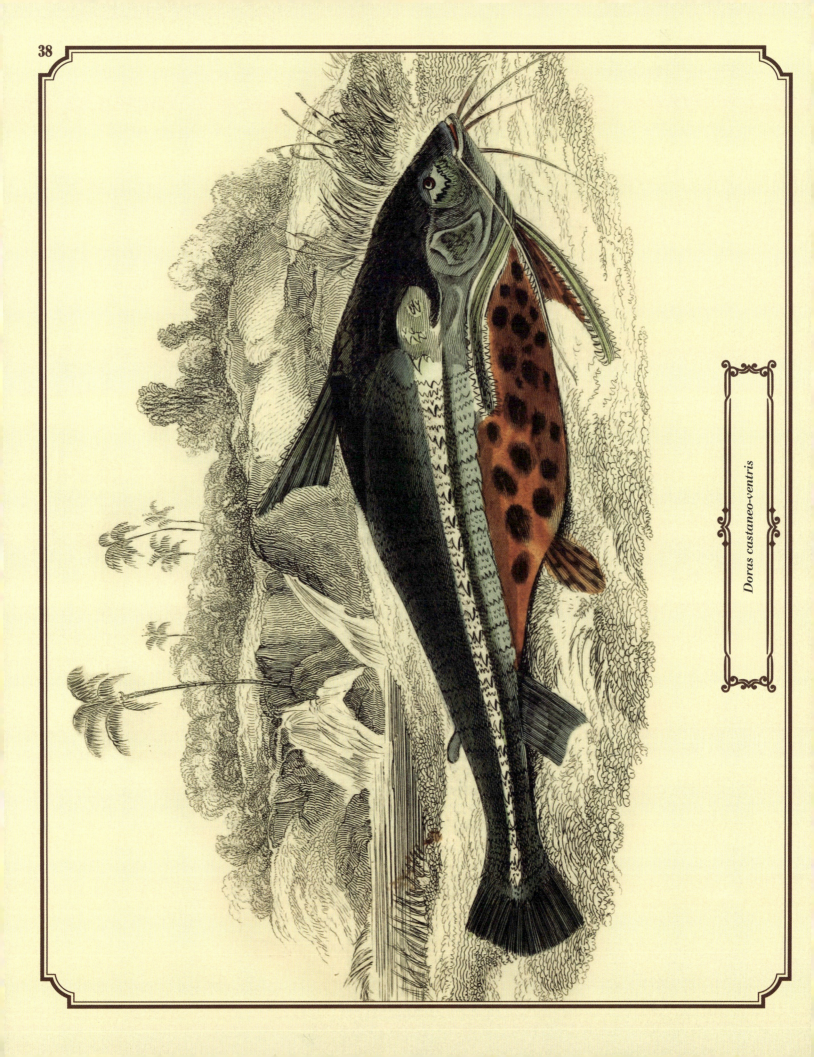

Doras castaneo-ventris

Brown Dorsal-striped Doras

Serrasalmo punctatus

Spotted Saw-bellied Salmon

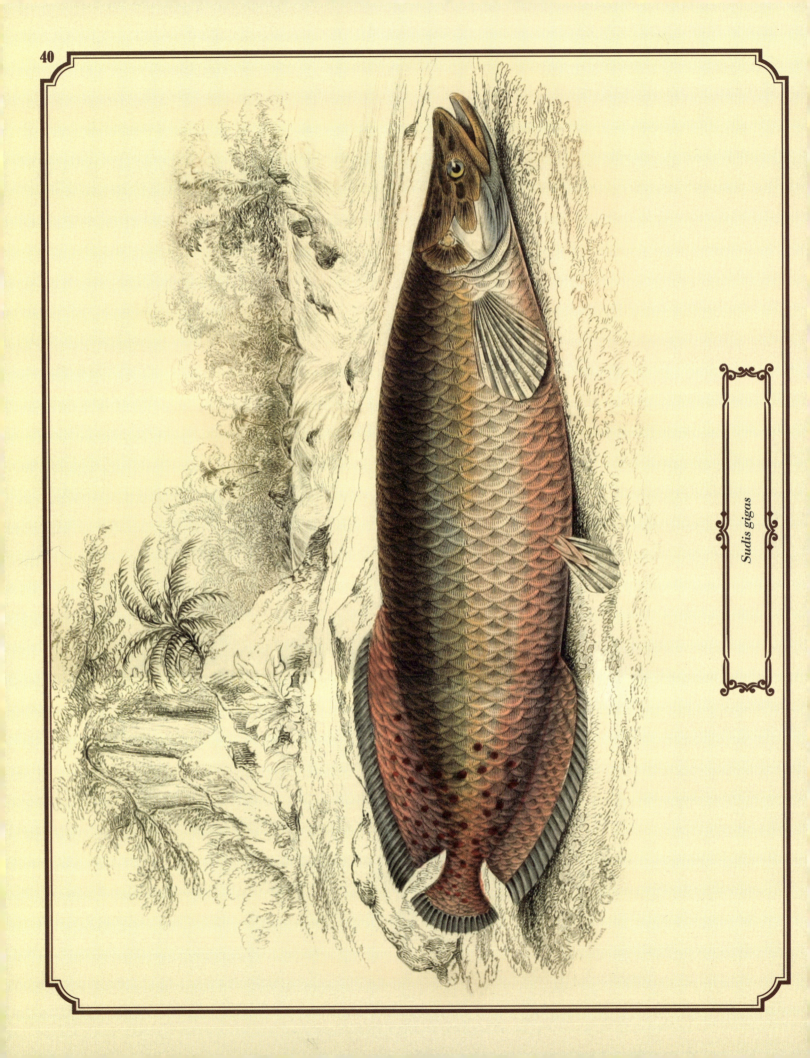
Sudis gigas

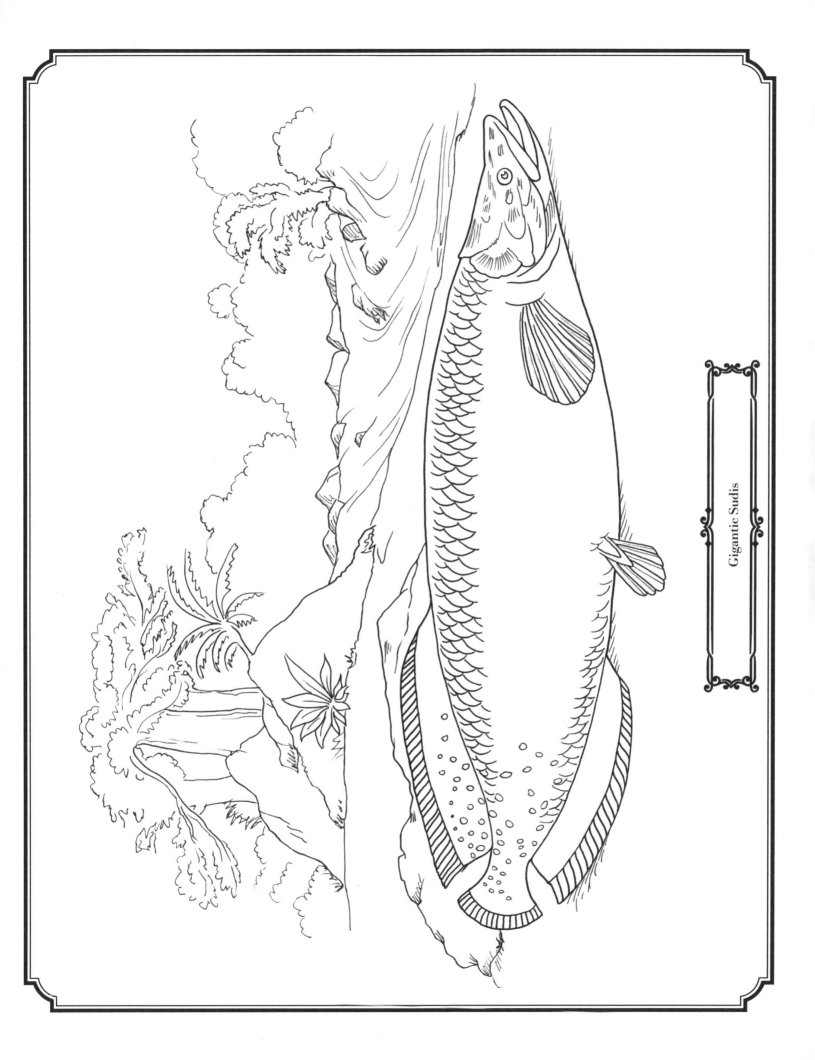

Gigantic Sudis

Gasterosteus spinosa

Fifteen-spined Stickleback nest and eggs

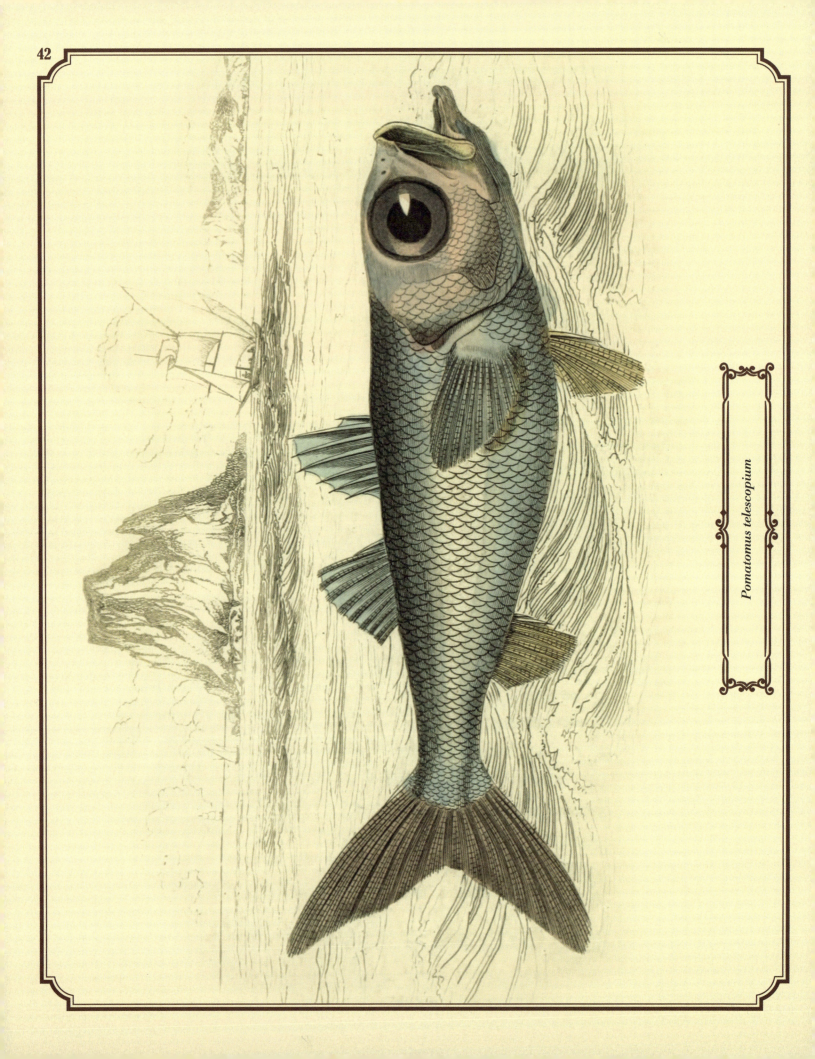

Pomatomus telescopium

43

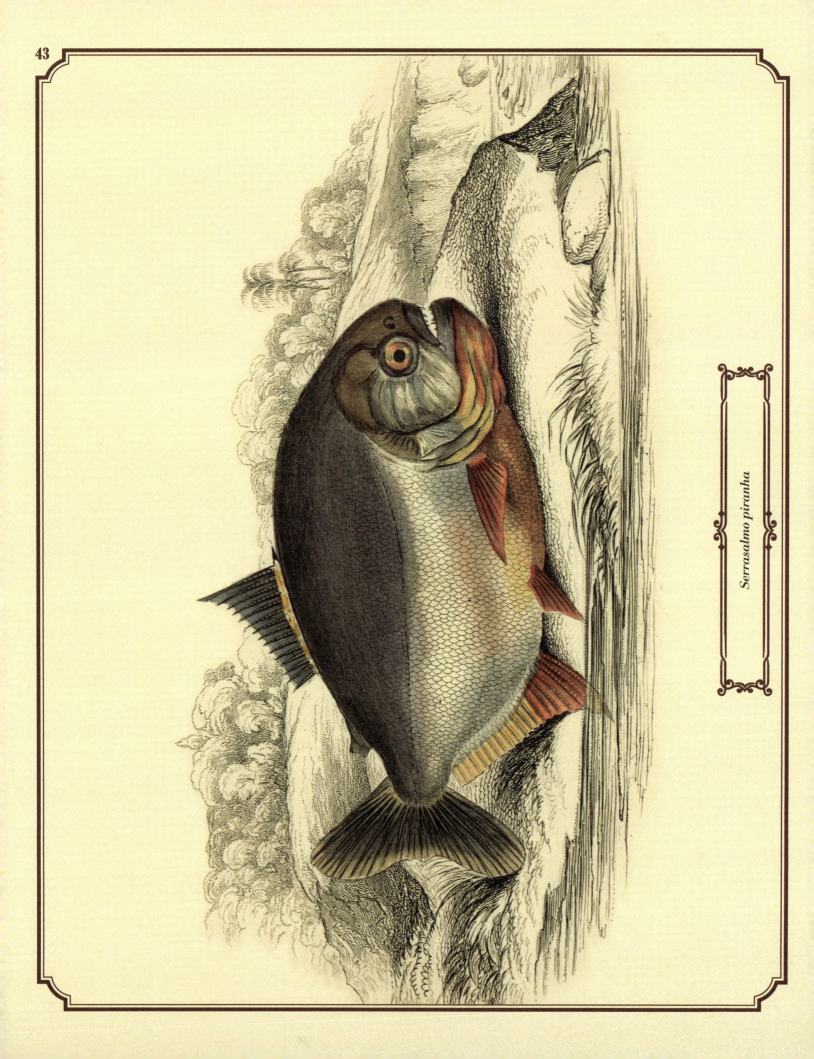

Serrasalmo piranha

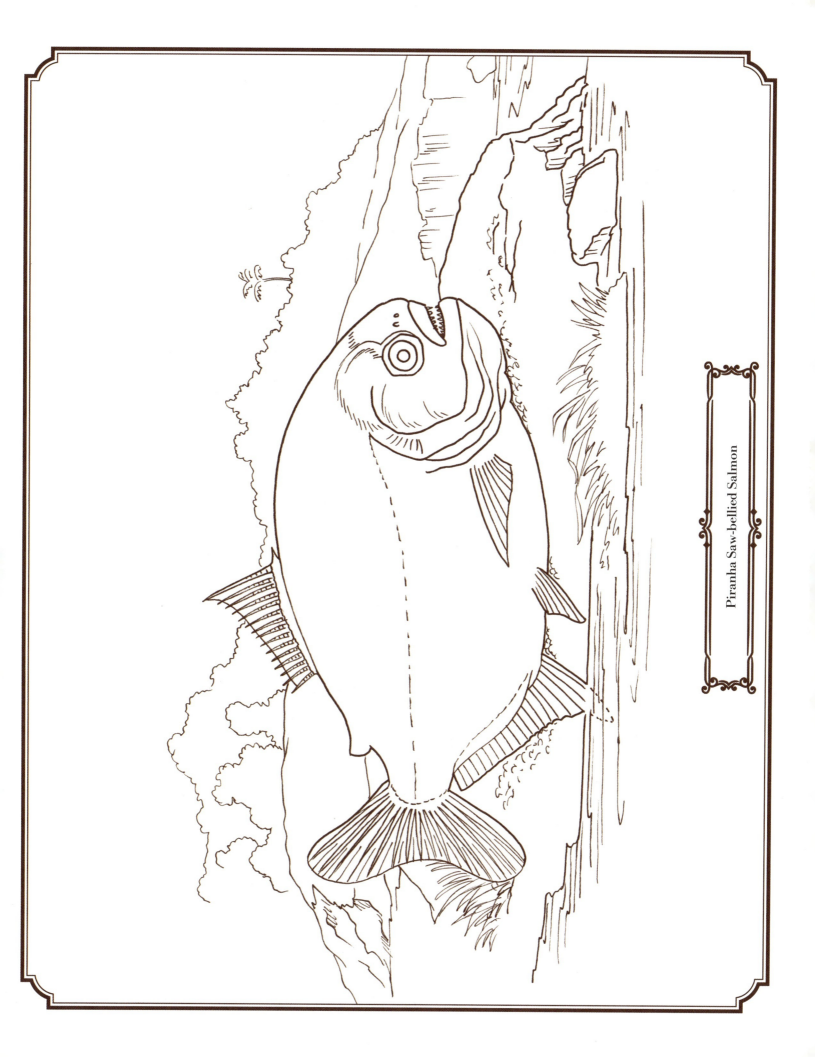

Piranha Saw-bellied Salmon

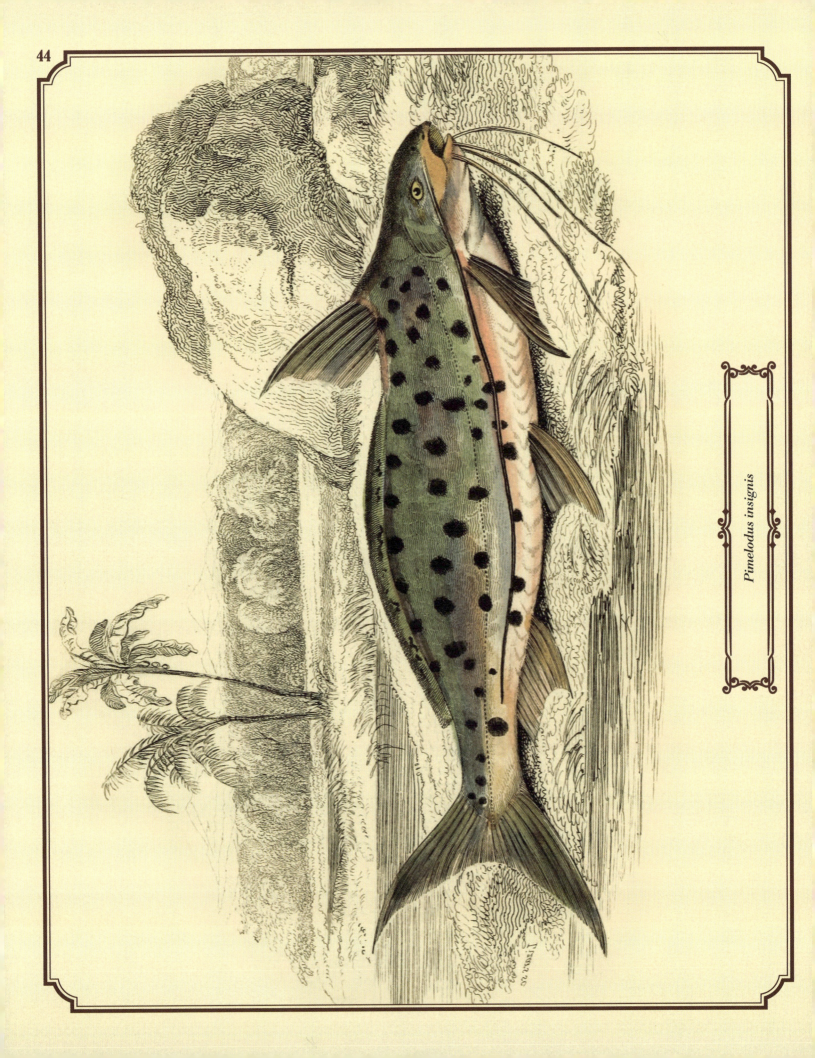

Pimelodus insignis

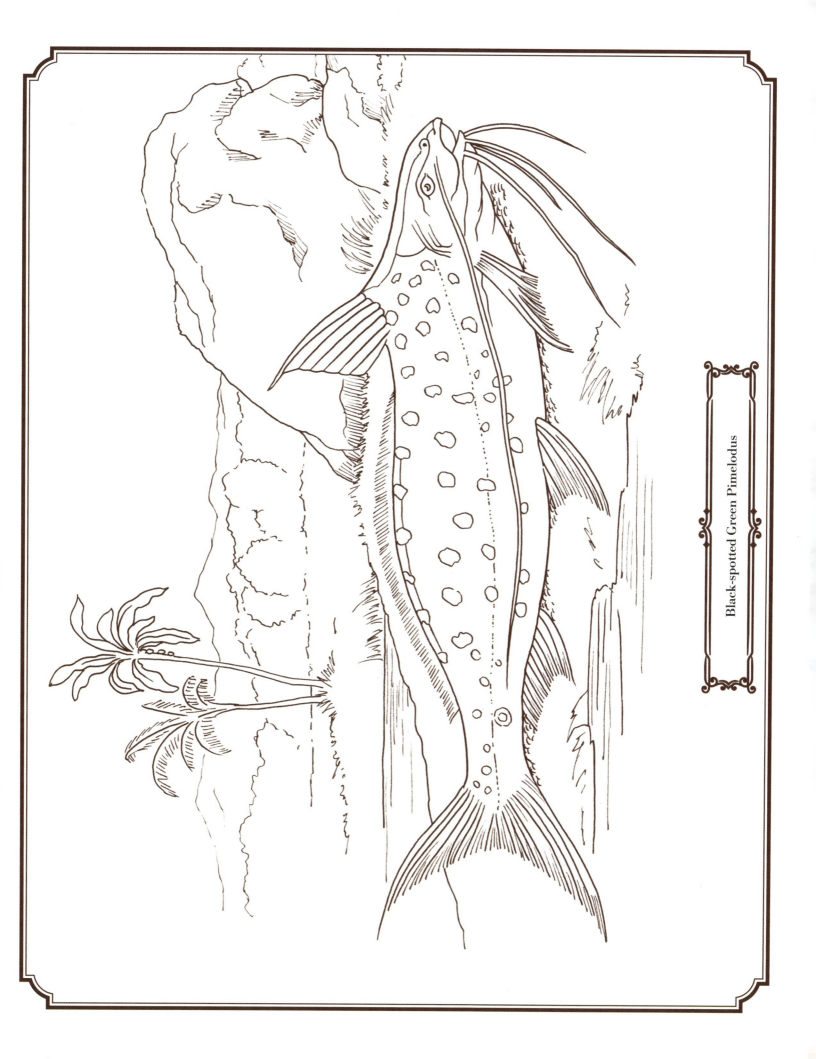
Black-spotted Green Pimelodus